"My heart hurt as I read *T.* candidly and honestly de childhood of the author. And I was dismayed as the pain and disappointment in my heart and head increased as I read how a child protective system and foster care further did not fulfill their goals as a shield of protection for one child, and I asked, "How many more?" My heart was lifted as the resilience, determination and faith of the author provided the springboard to thrive and success. All professionals, from the medical, social work, education and faith field should read *Twice Over a Man* ... this is real life for too many children, and we must recognize this so they to can thrive."

—Carmen Schulze
Former State Director
Missouri Division of Family Services

"*Twice Over a Man* is more than a memoir—it's a blueprint for transformation. This book is essential for anyone facing personal challenges or at a crossroads. Orvin Kimbrough's journey from a traumatic childhood to a successful leader showcases resilience, determination, and faith in action. What sets this book apart is its practical wisdom, actionable strategies, and call to prayer. Whether overcoming adversity, seeking inspiration, or navigating life's complexities, this book offers invaluable insights and encouragement. Reading the book will leave you deeply moved and inspired to take control of your own story. It's a powerful reminder that with the right mindset and through the power of God and perseverance, you can achieve extraordinary things (Ephesians 3:20)."

—David Steward
Founder and Chairman
World Wide Technology

"*Twice Over a Man* is the love letter to the World we didn't know we needed. But Orvin did. By bravely sharing his story, Orvin takes a deep dive into the power of the human spirit's ability to overcome and thrive. The book is perfectly paced, providing a raw look into his childhood, while connecting the reader with how he grew from repeated, harmful experiences, eventually becoming the CEO of two of the US's most innovative institutions: the United Way of Greater St. Louis and Midwest BankCentre. Orvin's memoir also highlights sweeping and riveting connections to historical and current racial justice and economic inequities, providing meaningful insight on how to right these societal wrongs. In the end, Orvin's love letter tells each of us what we need to hear: we can – and must – defeat adversity in order to live a life truly worth living."

—**Melanie Scheetz**
Executive Director
Foster & Adoptive Care Coalition

"*Twice Over a Man* is moving, powerful, simultaneously draining and inspiring. It made me reflect on Viktor Frankl's *Man's Search for Meaning*. No matter the circumstances, any person can decide what will become of them mentally and spiritually. It made me think: what could you have accomplished if you had been born into and surrounded by the opportunities others take for granted or squander? This memoir evoked deep emotions, making me feel that no child should have to endure such pain and turmoil, even if it seeds resilience and drive that fuels future success. It compels me to never let a child give up on themselves and encourages readers to reflect on their own opportunities and resilience."

—**Milton J. Little Jr.**
President & CEO
United Way of Greater Atlanta

"Orvin's memoir, *Twice Over a Man,* is a visceral and raw account of resilience in the face of systemic failures. His story vividly highlights the persistent issues within the foster care system and generational poverty. It's a must-read for leaders investing in system change. The book raises critical questions about the support structures and resilience factors that can make a difference. Orvin's courage and vulnerability offer valuable insights for driving meaningful change and improving the lives of those in similar situations."

—James Berges and Elizabeth Mannen Berges

"*Twice Over a Man* by Orvin Kimbrough takes you on the inspiring if sometimes hard to read journey from being born into abject poverty, living in an abusive home, and through the foster care system until he became a successful businessman and community leader. See how the principles he lives by, like perseverance, hard work, positivity, and faith helped him achieve this outcome. If Orv can do it, so can you."

—Clif Smart
Emeritus President
Missouri State University

"I first came to know Orv Kimbrough as one of the most impressive young professionals I had ever met. Now knowing his entire back story and early journey to becoming that successful young man explains it all. This book is both inspiration and road map for anyone who first needs to survive and then dream to thrive."

—Brian Gallagher
Former Chief Executive Officer
United Way Worldwide

"*Twice Over a Man* is the compelling tale of a young boy, raised in troubled families, distressed communities, and a greater society that seemed not prepared to care for his welfare. Readers will instantly love young Orv and hearts will ache to show him the affection and guidance that all children deserve. Others will be surprised to know that Orv, the young man, grew to be a faithful leader in his community and state who, through the fire and anguish of his adverse childhood experiences, was able to pen 'The Thrivers Toolkit: Personal Growth Principles' that would benefit anyone who cares for children or who may be on their own self-reflection journey. The poems and meditations affirm that "against all odds, achieving the unthinkable is within our grasp."

—Dwayne Proctor, Ph.D.
President & CEO
Missouri Foundation for Health

"As I read *Twice Over a Man*, I often felt I was peering into the author's life, particularly his childhood, and I felt both humbled and horrified. It is like reading his diary or peeking inside a window to some of his most heartbreaking and formative experiences. I felt sadness for him. I worried for him. I feared for him. I cried for him. I felt joy for him. I celebrated him. Somehow, I never felt sorry or pity for him. I felt hope. His resilience was like a steady drumbeat. The light just keeps breaking through...his light could not and did not dim. He just kept turning so little into so much, creating a platform from which to make the next leap. There is a mix of old soul maturity with lighthearted positivity and humor that feels so authentic to the author's writing. The poetry is powerful! It could have been a book of poems. The quotes and those quoted are thoughtful as well. Wow!"

—Michele Holton

"I was deeply moved by the inspiring memoir; *Twice Over a Man* that takes readers on a journey of resilience, hope, and determination. Orvin T. Kimbrough's story of overcoming adversity and rising above the challenges of growing up abused and orphaned at a young age is both heart-wrenching and uplifting. Orvin sheds light on the constants that helped shape his life and offers valuable insights and lessons for anyone facing their own struggles. This book is a must-read for those who believe in the power of perseverance and the potential for greatness in us all."

—Suzanne King
President & CEO
Mental Health America of Eastern Missouri

"The first time I met Orvin Kimbrough through a mutual friend, I thought: either this guy is the biggest and most persuasive fraud I have ever met, or he is truly remarkable, one in a million. Over the years, and after reading the manuscript of this book, I came to realize that he is unlike anybody I have ever met. He is no fraud. Indeed, as he says in the book, he 'shows up with his whole self.' Orvin came through a traumatic childhood in St. Louis and learned everything the hard way—by trial and error. Yet, he managed to transcend the hardship, hunger, and abuse he experienced and become an extraordinary citizen. This book reminds me that despite all evidence to the contrary, hope lives. It is a must-read for people who grew up in the kind of background Orvin did and aspire to do more."

—Fr Charles Bouchard OP
Senior Fellow and former president
Aquinas Institute of Theology St, Louis.

"*Twice Over a Man* is an extraordinary journey of trial and triumph through faith, perseverance, and hard work. Through his insightful, emotional, and inspiring story, Orvin Kimbrough gives us the motivation to stay the course and embrace the journey—a powerful imperative!"

—Tara Perry
Chief Executive Officer
National CASA/GAL Association

"*Twice Over a Man* is a raw, emotional, brave, and unfiltered memoir. For those who believe there is no hope, Orvin's life story demonstrates that it is possible to overcome insurmountable odds and live a life of purpose, success, and healing. *Twice Over a Man* is a once in a generation book. It is not an exaggeration to say that this book will change and save lives."

—Miller W. Boyd, III Ph.D.
Historian

TWICE OVER
A MAN

TWICE OVER A MAN

*A Fierce Memoir of an Orphan Boy
Who Doggedly Determined a Finer Life*

ORVIN T. KIMBROUGH

Stonebrook Publishing
Saint Louis, Missouri

A STONEBROOK PUBLISHING BOOK
©2024 Orvin Kimbrough
This book was guided in development and edited
by Nancy L. Erickson,
https://nancylerickson.com

Scripture quotations are from The ESV® Bible (The Holy Bible,
English Standard Version®), © 2001 by Crossway, a publishing
ministry of Good News Publishers. Used by permission.
All rights reserved.

Library of Congress Control Number: 2024909083

Softcover ISBN: 978-1-955711-34-0
eBook ISBN: 978-1-955711-35-7

www.stonebrookpublishing.net

PRINTED IN THE UNITED STATES OF AMERICA

To the fatherless and motherless, to the seemingly rudderless—this book is for the survivors who have felt overlooked at every stage of their journey. It stands as a testament to the heights we can reach when we commit to resilience and allow ourselves to dream big.

CONTENTS

PROLOGUE

Over the past thirty years, many people have confided in me and told me about their traumas. I think they were drawn to me because I've been transparent in sharing my own traumatic experiences. Research shows that about 70 percent of Americans have dealt with trauma. It affects every aspect of our lives and leaves us unoptimized, even though we sometimes achieve outward success. Interpersonal trauma makes it harder to maintain genuine relationships.

The question I'm most frequently asked is, "How did you make it?" Answering that question has been a lifelong endeavor. Sometimes my response is that mentally, I am still making it—I haven't yet made it. Other times, my answer is as simple as, "I had to get up and face life every day, with no guarantees, and agree to give it one more day." People ask this because of the outward success they see in me. I remind them that many of us show signs of outward success while struggling internally. Hard work and a strong work ethic, whether applied to achieving external goals or repairing ourselves internally, are fundamentally the same. A strong work ethic doesn't guarantee success, although it does increase your odds of achievement. Motion of any type is a sign that you are alive, whether it is forward, backward, or just walking in place.

I had to establish constants in my life: firm actions and attitudes that helped me develop into the man I am today. These constants include a growth mindset (even when growth meant standing still or going backward), an outstretched arm seeking help, prayer, finding ways around barriers, and pruning relationships based on the age and stage of life.

In these pages, I hope to shed light on the constants that helped me navigate my journey and to offer a roadmap for others who are trying to find their way. My story is one of resilience, hope, and the unwavering belief that no matter where we start or what we go through, we have the power to change our trajectory. It's a tale of perseverance, faith, and the relentless pursuit of a better future.

I struggled to write this book. I first thought about writing my life story when I was in my twenties, nearly thirty years ago. I wasn't a stranger to writing and storytelling. As a teenager, I was in a conscious rap group called Young Black Intelligence (YBI), and we spent hours crafting our message and our music and managing our performances for talent shows throughout the Saint Louis area. But writing a book is a different beast altogether, and I was derailed time and time again.

I was derailed by a lack of confidence, both in myself and from others. Early on, I was told that I needed more life experience to write my story, so I stood down. I struggled to commit the necessary time to the project and to deal with resurfacing traumas that I hadn't fully addressed. I believe some traumas are never fully resolved; you are always in the process of dealing with them. I also believe that time is our most important commodity, and to complete this book, I had to isolate myself, foregoing social and other gatherings. My friends and family bore the brunt of my absences as I balanced this full-time endeavor with my business and community service pursuits.

Further, I lacked a system to approach the project and had too many ideas. I had to adopt a disciplined approach where I shared only the defining moments that make up who I am today. This book isn't meant to cover my entire life, just my first twenty-five years! My defining moments can be divided into three eight-year chunks: my first eight years that ended with my mom's death, my next eight years in foster care, and my final eight years of growing into a young adult, taking control, and getting married.

Despite all my so-called achievements, I still have moments where I question my success—perhaps a bit of imposter syndrome. Writing this book has been partly therapeutic and has helped me make sense of my journey and recognize my resilience. My story represents the belief that no matter the starting point, we all have the power to shape our future.

I speak transparently and honestly about my traumas because I believe that embracing this openness is freeing for all of us who strive to reach the next level of personal and professional success. By not being slaves to our past, we can use past hurts as a source of strength and momentum.

I share with you the more private Orvin and include my views on relationships, which are key to everything I do. I often commingle business and personal aspects because I can't compartmentalize who I am as a person. This is how I've chosen to live my life. I show up with my whole self, no matter the environment.

I also reflect on my communities—East Saint Louis, North Saint Louis, and more. I express my thoughts about public policies that shaped my upbringing and about race relations, especially the intense period during my college years. I am not a sociologist or an historian, so these reflections are not intended to be scholarly.

As a kid, I lived in a rough environment that included violence, domestic abuse, physical abuse, sexual abuse, sexual assault, and foul language. Throughout the book, I worked hard to remain honest to those experiences. The early chapters are raw and reflect that reality. I sometimes use harsh words and images. In this project, I share aspects of my child development and sexuality as I developed into a young adult.

I know about poverty and overcoming it. As I peel back the many layers of this project, I aim to connect my past to how we help those at the economic bottom gain insight and encouragement to find pathways up. It's also about helping those at the economic top gain perspective about their position and what they can do to be helpful.

My ultimate goal in writing this book is to encourage people by using my life story as a demonstration project. The principles found throughout this book are not just important for a survivor's toolkit; they are crucial for those seeking a thriver's toolkit.

Here are the principles I learned, without which I could not have become who that I am today. Look for these throughout the book, in the stories I tell and in the obstacles I've overcome, so you can apply them to your own life situations.

THE THRIVERS TOOLKIT: PERSONAL GROWTH PRINCIPLES

1. EMBRACE ADVERSITY AS AN OPPORTUNITY FOR GROWTH.

Despite numerous challenges, see adversity as a catalyst for your personal and professional growth, using each obstacle as a stepping stone to build resilience and strength.

Daily Meditation: *Despite the challenges, I will push beyond expectations and turn adversity into growth.*

2. FORGIVE AND LET GO OF PAST GRIEVANCES TO MOVE FORWARD.

By forgiving those who wronged you, you will free yourself from the burden of bitterness, allowing you to focus on positive future endeavors.

Daily Meditation: *I will let go of bitterness today by practicing forgiveness, so I can free myself to focus on the future.*

3. BE RESILIENT, DETERMINED, AND PERSISTENT IN THE FACE OF SETBACKS.

Your determination to succeed despite frequent changes and challenges will hone your resilience. The key to overcoming difficulties and achieving your goals is to stay persistent through difficulties. Commit to your path, even when it seems impossible, and your dedication will eventually lead to success.

Daily Meditation: *I will maintain unwavering focus and resilience today and will persistently bounce back from setbacks with determination.*

4. BUILD AND RELY ON A STRONG SUPPORT SYSTEM.

Recognize the importance of community and coaching. Connect with people and organizations that provide positive reinforcement. Draw strength from supportive individuals who encourage and support you.

Daily Meditation: *Today, I will draw strength from my supportive community, advisors, and positive connections.*

5. ENGAGE IN SELF-DISCOVERY TO UNDERSTAND YOUR STRENGTHS AND WEAKNESSES.

Reflect on your experiences so you can understand and embrace your uniqueness, which will lead to a stronger sense of self and direction.

Daily Meditation: *I will discover and embrace my unique strengths today.*

6. COMMIT TO HARD WORK AND DEDICATION.

Your relentless work ethic, exemplified by diligently working and balancing multiple responsibilities, underscores the importance of perseverance in achieving success.

Daily Meditation: *I will let perseverance and hard work drive my achievements today.*

7. EMBRACE CHANGE AND VIEW IT AS A PATH TO GROWTH.

Adapt to new environments and experiences so you can grow and discover new opportunities.

Daily Meditation: *I will embrace change today to unlock growth opportunities.*

8. FIND INNER PEACE THROUGH PRAYER AND MINDFULNESS.

Practicing prayer and mindfulness will provide you with the clarity and tranquility needed to handle life's ups and downs with a steady heart. Prayer can be a source of comfort and strength, and can help you find inner peace and maintain a balanced perspective.

Daily Meditation: *I will cultivate calmness and clarity through prayer and mindfulness today, seeking inner peace to calmly navigate my challenges.*

9. RECOGNIZE AND CELEBRATE YOUR SELF-WORTH BY SEEING YOURSELF AS GOD SEES YOU.

Acknowledge your inherent value based on how God sees you rather than the world's standards. Set healthy boundaries about who you let speak into your life, so you can make decisions that honor your self-worth and boost your confidence.

Daily Meditation: *I will honor my self-worth today by setting healthy boundaries and seeing myself as God sees me.*

10. FACE AND OVERCOME YOUR FEARS.

Confront your fears, such as public speaking and difficult subjects, to demonstrate your courage and unlock new possibilities. Speaking words of life, overcoming, and growth will help you face and overcome these fears.

Daily Meditation: *I will unlock new possibilities today by confronting my fears and speaking words of life, overcoming, and growth.*

11. SEEK AND VALUE MENTORSHIP.

Learning from mentors and sponsors will provide you with wisdom and guidance and will play a crucial role in your personal and professional development.

Daily Meditation: *I will gain wisdom and guidance from my mentors today.*

12. Prioritize Education and Embrace Lifelong Learning.

You must value education and continuously seek knowledge to open doors to new opportunities and equip you with essential skills for your journey. Lifelong learning and acquiring new knowledge and skills will ensure that you remain capable and prepared for future challenges.

Daily Meditation: *I will stay prepared for the future by valuing education and continuous learning today.*

13. Maintain a Positive Attitude, Even During Tough Times.

Your optimism and hopeful outlook, especially during challenging periods, will inspire those around you and reinforce your resilience.

Daily Meditation: *I will inspire resilience in myself and others today through optimism.*

14. Set Clear Goals and Plan for the Future.

Creating and pursuing well-defined goals will keep you focused and motivated, and will turn your dreams into achievable realities.

Daily Meditation: *I will transform dreams into reality today by setting clear goals.*

15. Practice Gratitude Regularly.

Expressing gratitude for the small and big things in life will bring you joy and contentment, enhancing your overall well-being.

Daily Meditation: *I will enhance my well-being today by practicing gratitude.*

16. GIVE BACK TO THE COMMUNITY.

Volunteering and helping others will enrich your life and create a positive impact on your community.

Daily Meditation: *I will create a positive impact today by giving back to my community.*

17. DEVELOP STRONG LEADERSHIP SKILLS.

Leading by example, communicating effectively, and inspiring others are essential aspects of your leadership journey. By practicing self-awareness and self-regulation, you can enhance your emotional intelligence and better motivate and guide those around you.

Daily Meditation: *I will inspire and guide others today by practicing self-awareness and self-regulation, strengthening my leadership through emotional intelligence.*

18. INVEST IN HEALTHY RELATIONSHIPS.

Investing in healthy relationships will provide you with support, love, and encouragement, and will make your journey more meaningful and fulfilling.

Daily Meditation: *I will find support and fulfillment today by nurturing healthy relationships.*

19. BELIEVE IN A POSITIVE FUTURE.

Believing in a positive future, even in the face of adversity, will help you stay focused on your goals and inspire others to do the same.

Daily Meditation: *I will stay focused on my goals today by believing in a positive future.*

20. EMBRACE VULNERABILITY TO BUILD GENUINE CONNECTIONS.

By being open and honest about your struggles, you will foster deeper connections with others and find strength in your authenticity.

Daily Meditation: *I will build genuine connections today by embracing vulnerability.*

21. HAVE FAITH IN YOURSELF AND YOUR JOURNEY.

Having faith in your abilities and trusting the process will give you the confidence to face challenges and move forward with conviction.

Daily Meditation: *I will trust my abilities and the process today to navigate challenges confidently.*

22. CELEBRATE BOTH YOUR WINS AND YOUR LOSSES.

Recognizing and celebrating all aspects of your journey, including your successes and failures, will help you appreciate your progress and learn from your experiences.

Daily Meditation: *Despite where I am, I have come so far and must appreciate my journey by celebrating both wins and losses.*

23. STEP OUT IN FAITH TO OVERCOME OBSTACLES.

Having faith in a higher power or in your own potential can provide the strength and courage needed to overcome life's obstacles. Let your faith guide you through difficult times.

Daily Meditation: *I will step out in faith today, trusting that I have the strength to overcome any obstacle.*

THESE PRINCIPLES FOR SUCCESS REFLECT the strategies that guided me throughout my journey, and they represent how I made it through various challenges and achieved my goals. As you begin reading this book, I hope these reflections resonate with you and inspire you to embrace your own journey with resilience, hope, and determination.

Remember, no matter where you start, you have the power to shape your future and make a difference in your life and the lives of others.

Please visit orvinkimbrough.com to sign up for our newsletter, to keep in touch, or to ask questions. Thank you for purchasing this book and writing a public review!

DISCLAIMER

This book is my story as I remember it. It is not intended to disparage or defame any individuals, living or deceased. Some of the names have been changed either because I cannot remember them accurately or for other personal reasons. While I have made every effort to present an accurate portrayal of my experiences, memory is fallible, and others may have different recollections of the events described.

The content in this book includes descriptions of violence, domestic abuse, sexual abuse, and other sensitive topics. Reader discretion is advised. The views and opinions expressed are my own and do not necessarily reflect those of any organizations or individuals mentioned. This book is not intended to serve as legal, medical, or professional advice. Readers seeking assistance or counseling for similar issues should consult a qualified professional.

END OF THE TUNNEL

Though there is pain
there is light at the end of the tunnel
though the road seems obscure at times
I encourage you from the heart of the struggle
where I've gone some would say
many don't make it back
and if they do they dare not speak
of the horrible detailed facts
there are opportunistic thieves in this world
that will rob you of your joy
and violate you in every imaginable way
till your life seems without purpose
and your will is all but destroyed
what gave you the strength to come this far
despite the tears you've cried
and once you identify what that was
use it as your guide
though there is pain
there is light at the end of the tunnel
though the road seems obscure at times
I encourage you from the heart of the struggle.

CHAPTER 1

"Obstacles don't have to stop you.
If you run into a wall, don't turn around and give up.
Figure out how to climb it, go through it, or work around it."

—*Michael Jordan*

I've been driven to achieve for most of my life. Perhaps this was a function of not being born with much. Perhaps it was a function of not growing up with much. It's surely a function of how I think I was perceived from early on. Whatever the case, I've been single-minded in my focus on doing more than what was expected of me. In 2014, United Way of Greater Saint Louis—where I was in my first year as president and CEO—hosted a private charity event that all members of the then Saint Louis Rams football team and their coaching staff attended. It was special because, outside of official team business, this was a rare occurrence. It seemed like there were thousands of fans in attendance.

We invited high school students from across the Saint Louis region to attend the event at America's Center, the largest event space in our city. As I made my way around to each table, which had an NFL player as its main attraction, I met a young man who attended one of our North County high schools. He was in his junior year. I asked him the same question I asked every young person in attendance.

"What do you plan to do after high school?" I asked.

He said that he wasn't sure because he was only an average student. I told him that I, too, had been only an average student, and at times, I was below average. Then, in a rare showing of hubris or pride, I told him that I was the leader of the group hosting the event that day. He was shocked. It wasn't the first time my title or accomplishments would shock people, nor would it be the last. However, it was an impactful moment. In real time, I saw how my success could affect someone who'd counted himself out and could help him reimagine his life going forward.

As I think about my life, what I needed from the start more than anything else was simply a chance. In June of 2013, when I was named CEO of United Way, I told a group I belonged to that I was fortunate the organization took the risk on me.

The only other guy in the group, Chris, said, "You aren't the risk you think you are."

He went on to explain that I'd done well with every opportunity I'd pursued up to that point, so the odds were now in my favor. The idea of *favor* is how I got comfortable with the fact that I'd succeeded more often than not as an adult. God's favor, or grace, is God giving us the ability to do something that is humanly impossible for us to do. In my view, God's favor is often activated on the other side of hard work and effort.

My faith, hard work, effort, and luck have taken me on an incredible journey, and I've met amazing people along the way. Some are resigned to earning a good living to benefit their families and perpetuate their legacies, while others are motivated by a sense of responsibility that comes with privilege or enlightened self-interest to benefit others. One approach is more akin to supporting people marginally, and the other is more akin to helping monumentally. The distinction between marginal and monumental benefits became significant for me. When I meet people who are generally more self-centered, I often find that they want the "poor person" and the subject of their support to be marginally successful—they help, but only to a certain limit. In contrast, there are those who are "others focused," who understand that there is enough and believe that having power, money, and influence is okay and feel better when used to help others. They genuinely want to extend a helping hand or offer a ladder to economic opportunity and generational hope. These are two different approaches, but no matter the approach, if you need help, both can be valuable tools.

I COULDN'T BELIEVE IT. With two-year-old Maddison—my firstborn—in tow, I sat in a meeting inside a large, colorful home in Ladue, Missouri, one of the wealthiest zip codes in America. The homeowner was a White woman who was telling me about what poor Black children needed to overcome their poverty. In between her asking me about the texture of my daughter's hair and her style of pigtails, I tried to give her a perspective. However, she dismissed me as being uninformed and disconnected from poverty. She was a bulldog in her approach and delivery, and she said in half jest, "It's been a while since you've been poor."

She was correct. At that point, I'd achieved several advanced degrees and was gainfully employed at a nonprofit earning a "massive" $40,000 annually; I could be characterized as lower-middle class.

I kept myself buttoned up as I listened to this woman who, in my mind, subscribed to an outdated nineteenth-century "noblesse oblige" approach of serving people who were born into economically starved neighborhoods, born into generational poverty, born into sexual and physical abuse, born into an underfunded education system that wasn't designed for most people to move up the economic ladder—who was not just *born into* but *raised* in toxic trauma and stress that resulted from living in high-crime environments and growing up in the foster care system intended to stabilize your trauma rather than launch you into becoming the leader of the second-largest privately held bank in the market. I am all those things—and this is my story.

When you don't come from much or have access to much, you learn to be scrappy. Everything becomes a tool. I was a scrappy kid. I used what I had to accomplish what I wanted. I had anger issues, so I had to learn how to use anger. I had trust issues, so I had to learn in what ways I could trust to accomplish things with and through other people, things that couldn't be done solo. "Scrappy," as defined by the *Merriam-Webster Dictionary*, is "having an aggressive and determined spirit." Scrappy is never taking no for an answer. Scrappy means getting back up if you get knocked down. It's being mentally tough and creative to find solutions. Scrappy is a "keep fighting" attitude.

When you don't come from much or have access to much, you learn to be scrappy.

Scrappy acknowledges that setbacks are inevitable, but failure is not an option. I didn't have many options as a kid. If I was going to survive, it was up to me.

IT WAS A COLD SUNDAY NIGHT on December 17, 2006, just days before my thirty-first birthday and the start of my unlikely journey as an executive with United Way of Greater Saint Louis. It was a season of transition and reflection. I sat back in my beige, faux-leather recliner to enjoy one of my favorite pastimes: watching *60 Minutes*. On that Sunday, one of the segments was called "Lost and Found." Correspondent Daniel Schorr set up the story with these words:

> They've been called some of the loneliest people on earth: children who were taken away from their parents due to neglect or abuse but were never adopted by new families. Stranded in the child welfare system, they move from foster homes to group homes. There are tens of thousands of these children. They have no one—not a single relative to visit on Christmas or their birthday.

This seemed eerily close to my story. Then, anchor Lesley Stahl told the story of a nonprofit organization that was using a model called "family finding" to help foster kids find family members. With the help of technology, the nonprofit finds the relatives and adults who became estranged from the child and who are willing to come back into their lives.

Stahl's story triggered me. As a foster child myself, I knew it was common for children who were removed from their birth families to never know their lineage. It had been a decade since I'd aged out of the foster care system, but I'd never lost the desire to know from whom and from where I came. I'd barely known my mother, who died at twenty-eight, nor did I know my father. I also knew that foster kids like me would often meditate on fantasies and imagine things that were seemingly impossible or improbable. Could this process and technology help me, or had I been dreaming?

I went over to my desktop computer, found an ancestry. com-type site, and paused. The site needed a few data points about my early life.

What's your mother's name? *Carolyn Kimbrough*, I typed. What's your father's name? I thought for a moment. I never knew my father, but I'd been told that I was named after him.

17

So, I pounded, as if screaming my name—no, *his* name—into the keyboard: *ORVIN*. I didn't know his last name. Continuing on, I shared that I was born in East Saint Louis, Illinois, and had residences on the Missouri side of the Mississippi River. Within minutes, the site produced a possible match for my father, complete with family history and contact information.

How could this be? I was paralyzed and stared at the computer screen as if it had somehow wronged me. Over the next day, I went back and forth through a range of emotions—from sadness, through resentment, to happiness, and back again. I finally decided that the first course of action was to ask a police officer friend if there was a way to check whether this guy had a criminal past. I was more interested in whether there was a history of violence or sexual crimes. I had a wife and small children and was not about to invite that spirit into my home. He got back to me quickly and indicated that he'd found a misdemeanor weapons charge, but that was the extent of it. I was still mentally foggy at that point. Going from identifying with no one to possibly having a father in a matter of seconds was frankly overwhelming.

As I scanned the list and the accompanying telephone numbers, my eyes settled on a name: Wanda, identified as Orvin's sister. With a mixture of anticipation and uncertainty, I dialed her number. The ringing phone echoed in what felt like an extended moment of suspense.

She answered with a simple, "Hello?"

My response was initially silence. Words escaped me.

Finally, I managed to say, "Hello, my name is Orvin Kimbrough," my voice betraying the nervousness I felt, a nervousness so intense that I began to sweat despite the winter chill.

Almost instantly, she responded, "Carolyn Kimbrough's son?" It seemed she recognized the name, likely thanks to caller ID.

"Excuse me?" I replied, clinging to every word, prolonging the moment in my shock.

She explained, "I asked Orvin if he knew about you some time ago. We've been following your success in the *Saint Louis American*," referring to the local newspaper focused on the African American community.

Confusion and dismay washed over me, feelings I hadn't anticipated. As our conversation unfolded, Wanda expressed her pride in me, mentioned that my cousins were eager to meet me, and encouraged me to connect with my father. The term "your father" landed with unexpected weight. Until that point, I'd been navigating life quite independently and embarked on a path to survive and make a meaningful impact through my work at the United Way.

I ultimately reached out to Orvin and arranged to meet him at a coffee house in Ferguson, Missouri. I arrived a little early on the day we planned to meet, filled with anticipation. As he entered, I instinctively scanned his features, searching for any trace of resemblance to myself. However, no such similarities were immediately apparent. He was shorter than me, his skin a shade darker, and he lacked the pronounced curvature at the back of my head—a unique feature that, I was told, could have been the result of my mother not massaging my head enough as a baby to smooth out the lump, or perhaps it was a genetic trait inherited from my father. Despite these physical differences, our conversation flowed effortlessly. He warmly invited me to his home, where we delved deeper into our stories and sifted through photographs, connecting over shared histories and the stories they told.

Orvin resided in a quaint bungalow nestled within an inner-ring suburb of North Saint Louis County. His home was tidy and welcoming, a testament to his attention to detail. As we conversed, he bridged many gaps in stories I had either heard in fragments or barely remembered. Interestingly, he revealed that he had once dated a friend of my mom's. During a period when my mom was living with this friend, Orvin and my mom connected, which led to their brief relationship in the 1970s. He had no doubts about being my father and posited a compelling question: why else would my mom have given me his name if not to signify his undeniable connection to me?

The only thing that was certain now was that I was born in and shaped by the city of East Saint Louis.

I had a lot to think about when I went home that night. I'd been taken advantage of and disappointed so much in my life that it was so difficult for me to let others in—men, in particular. I called him after a few days and asked him to consent to a DNA test.

"It's expensive, and you're my son no matter what a test says," he answered.

I paid for the test, and it was conclusive that Orvin was not my father. After telling him the news in January 2007, I never spoke to him again. The only thing that was certain now was that I was born in and shaped by the city of East Saint Louis.

YOU WON'T FIND ANY TRACE of the hospital where I was born, Christian Welfare Hospital, in East Saint Louis, Illinois. Like many landmarks in that community, it's been scraped away and is lost to time. The site at Martin Luther King Drive and 15th Street is now home to a housing development called Sinai Village in the city's Winstanley neighborhood. The surrounding land is flat, all the way across the Mississippi River to the Gateway Arch. Four attractive, suburban-style homes sit on the lot next to a neatly kept, multifamily brick building from another era. Across 15th Street is a large vacant lot, no doubt the former home of other buildings, marked by a lone, rusted-out streetlamp. The streetlamp has no light fixture, and the intersection has no street signs.

In the early 20th century, Christian Welfare Hospital stood as one of only two medical institutions in East Saint Louis, alongside Saint Mary's Hospital. The year 1940 marked a significant milestone for Christian Welfare with the inauguration of a new facility, later subject to expansion. Within these walls, I entered the world on December 20, 1974. Fast forward twenty-five years, the hospital underwent a transformation, rebranding as Gateway Community Hospital. However, this new iteration lacked a crucial service: a maternity ward. As highlighted by Jonathan Kozol in his 1990 publication *Savage Inequalities: Children in America's Schools,* the stark reality was laid bare: "There is no place to have a baby in East Saint Louis."

In 1917, East Saint Louis was thrust into turmoil as mobs of White residents launched a violent assault on the city's African American community. This upheaval was precipitated by the arrival of Black migrants from the South, part of the Great Migration of the 1910s, which saw the city's African American population swell to nearly 12,000 people, doubling from 1910 to 1917. The spark of the violence was ignited in May when the Aluminum Ore Company enlisted Black workers to replace striking White employees. The situation escalated in early July following a tragic misunderstanding in which Black residents, mistaking them for hostile White assailants who had terrorized Black neighborhoods in June, fatally shot two White plainclothes police officers. This incident spurred the police to permit White rioters to exact vengeance on Black citizens.

Carlos Hurd, a reporter celebrated for his compelling coverage of the RMS Titanic's demise in 1912, offered a haunting portrayal of the events in East Saint Louis. His firsthand observations, featured in the *Saint Louis Post-Dispatch* and *The Crisis* magazine, depicted a chilling spectacle: "The East Saint Louis affair, as I saw it, was a manhunt, pursued with a veneer of sportiveness yet devoid of the fairness inherent in true sport. It was marked by a chilling precision and a perverse sense of enjoyment. 'Get a n*****' became a harrowing rallying cry, punctuated by the repeated demand, 'Get another!'"

According to Chris Lumpkins and others in the brochure "Sacred Sites: A Self-Guided Tour of the East St. Louis Race Riot," the riots permanently damaged the city. Black homes and businesses were burned to the ground. Seven thousand Black residents fled across the Mississippi River to Missouri, and many never returned. An unknown number of Blacks were killed through beatings, hangings, burnings, or shootings. Contemporary estimates of the Black death toll varied from thirty-nine (according to the US government) to over two hundred (according to the NAACP). However, the riots may have had another enduring effect that impacted thousands more. The city's burgeoning Black business and civic leadership was decimated, their assets stolen or destroyed, and many leaders were arrested. After the riots, the municipal government was restructured to reduce Black political influence in city governance.

As reported by Kenneth M. Reardon in "Back from the Brink: The East St. Louis Story," featured in *Gateway Heritage* during the winter of 1997–98, the city experienced a period of industrial prosperity in the 1940s and the post-World War II era. However, as industries began to relocate, the White, middle-class population also started to move away. This migration led to a dramatic demographic shift; over three decades, from 1960 to 1990, the city's White population plummeted from 55 percent to a mere 2 percent. Concurrently, the unemployment rate surged from 10 percent to 25 percent, which increased the rate of families living in poverty from 11 percent to 39 percent.

Reardon continued: the city's struggles were not limited to demographics. As they did in urban communities nationally, federal initiatives intended to help only worsened conditions. East Saint Louis became home to public housing projects that drove poor people into already poor neighborhoods as urban renewal and new highways started clearing away much of the existing infrastructure. Buildings like the Ainad Temple and the Art Deco Spivey Building still stand as monuments to the city's better days, but many—including the hospital where I was born—are long gone.

As Kenneth Reardon notes, "Between 1967 and 1991, the number of East Saint Louis-based businesses fell from 1,527 to 383, and the supply of local jobs dropped from 12,423 to 2,699." Real estate took a hit, too, causing the property tax base to drop by $400 million to only $162 million by 1991, while the city's debt climbed.

This was the world I was born into in 1974—a troubled community saddled with a national reputation for violence, drugs, poverty, and corruption. After my father left, my mother moved our family across the river to North Saint Louis. Like East Saint Louis, North City had become a mostly Black, economically poor, and historically rich area by that time. In our many apartments, but especially the one near Wabada and Arlington, I would learn more about survival, imagination, and its limits. I would learn about risk. I would learn even more about loss than I could

This was the world I was born into in 1974— a troubled community saddled with a national reputation for violence, drugs, poverty, and corruption.

ever imagine. However, I will always remember where I came from—a vanished hospital in a struggling, scrappy city with few street signs.

WHEN MY MOM MOVED MY THREE SIBLINGS and me to North Saint Louis City, we followed the steps of those who fled the race riots in 1917 across the Mighty Mississippi. You can't find a much bigger physical boundary than the Mississippi. Poet T. S. Eliot called it "a great brown god." Mark Twain said if you strained its water, you'd get an acre of soil. It defines the city of Saint Louis's eastern border and East Saint Louis's western border, carving out a gentle curve that inspired and reflects Eero Saarinen's Gateway Arch.

However, physical barriers can be overcome. In the nineteenth century, the Eads Bridge did the job. Then came the highways. Today, you can fly over the Mississippi without even noticing it. However, psychological boundaries are something else. Overcoming psychological boundaries—which the Mississippi has also been between Saint Louis and East Saint Louis for more than two hundred years—takes a lot more work. And unlike those brave workers who went underwater to sink the pylons for the Eads Bridge, the work needed to overcome psychological boundaries might go completely unnoticed—not invisible, but unnoticed.

As the city's Delmar Boulevard is sometimes called, the Delmar Divide is also a physical boundary with even more powerful psychological powers. Delmar is a major thoroughfare that runs west from downtown Saint Louis into Saint Louis County. It begins at Convention Plaza near the loading docks of America's Center, the city's largest convention facility. From there, it flows to the west through apartment complexes built in the 1990s that brought affordable housing to the city. Shortly after crossing Grand Avenue in the Grand Center Arts District—home of the Fox Theatre, Powell Hall, and the Contemporary Art Museum—Delmar makes a dogleg at one of the city's many private schools, Cardinal Ritter College Preparatory School. It picks up again at Vandeventer and continues, passing north of the city's fashionable Central West End and middle-class Skinker-DeBaliviere neighborhoods. Just across the city limits, it becomes the Delmar Loop, a funky stretch of restaurants, record stores, clothing boutiques, concert halls, a bowling alley, and, as of this writing, a bookstore. The "Loop" part is a throwback to when this stretch of Delmar was a major turnaround point for streetcars and is a favorite hangout for Washington University students. It recently became the home of upscale university housing. Going further west on Delmar takes you through the municipalities of University City, Clayton, and into Ladue, one of Saint Louis's—and the nation's—wealthiest suburbs. At Price Road, Delmar Boulevard ends.

Delmar has amazing powers. It gives mortal people the power to enter an entirely separate universe simply by walking across the street. In Saint Louis, "North City" means "north of Delmar." A demographic map of the city dramatically illustrates the contrast in racial composition—north of Delmar is virtually all-Black, and south of Delmar is largely White, especially further west. However, if you mapped other indicators, like access to banks, grocery stores, educational attainment, medical facilities, etc., you would quickly see that North City and South City are different worlds in other ways, too. In August 2014, Chico Harlan of the *Washington Post* described the two parallel universes:

> In the blocks to the immediate south: Tudor homes, wine bars, a racquet club, a furniture store selling sofas for $6,000. The neighborhood, according to U.S. Census data, is 70 percent White. In the blocks to the immediate north: knocked-over street signs, collapsing houses, fluttering trash, tree-bare streets with weeds blooming from the sidewalk. The neighborhood is 99 percent Black.

As a result, a lot of Saint Louisans have been conditioned to fear crossing that street from South City to North City. But for me and for much of my childhood, as well as parts of my adult life, North City was home.

Our situation was tough. We were extremely poor, and though I don't remember my mom working for any extended period, she did what she could to provide for us. The only thing I seemed to bring with me out of East Saint Louis was a powerful imagination. For young people, imagination is critical. It makes it possible to change the impossible, transform chaos into calm, and go places we may not be able to experience otherwise. I was in an economically challenged place, a place where poverty and crime flourished, but because of my imagination, I sometimes felt like I could do anything—even fly like Superman. In fact, I began to think that maybe I was Superman. It was a fantasy borne of feeling unloved by my mom, missing my dad, our poverty, our small one-bedroom apartment, our drug-infested North Saint Louis neighborhood, and our hunger. I needed this insulation from life's ails.

We had no food on many days, but not even hunger got in Superman's way. He was a bigger-than-life figure who had amazing powers that most children and adults were naturally drawn to. He could easily move a planet. He could travel faster than light. He had unlimited stamina. No food, no water, no rest, no problem! This often became my reality, and it was a problem. I admired the fact that Superman was invulnerable to all things—except, of course, Kryptonite.

To me, poverty—especially generational poverty—was like Kryptonite. It robbed people born with promise and potential of their intrinsic power, and we had plenty of poverty growing up in North City, on the wrong side of Delmar. Because of poverty, I was limited in what I could do. It weakened my power and had been imposed on me by my unlucky birth to a drug-addicted mom and an absent dad. Delmar's amazing power—its otherworldly ability to transport people from one universe to another—was part of the systemic racism that kept my family and our North City neighbors poor. I'm not making excuses; I'm just stating facts.

26

In 2013, a group of researchers at Washington University's Brown School and Saint Louis University, led by Brown School Associate Professor Jason Purnell, began studying the collective impact of poverty on Saint Louis's Black community. The study that resulted, "For the Sake of All," quantified for White Saint Louisans what Black Saint Louisans had known through experience for generations: living in North City was bad for your health, physically and psychologically. Some of the study's key findings are worth quoting at length:

> Residents of zip codes separated by only a few miles have up to an 18-year difference in life expectancy. Because of considerable residential segregation in Saint Louis, many areas with high African American populations are also areas with concentrated poverty and poor health. These neighborhoods often lack resources like healthy foods, safe green spaces for recreation, and convenient access to medical care.
>
> Education is one of the strongest and most consistent predictors of health, and gaps in life expectancy between those with low and high levels of education are widening. . . One in 10 African Americans in grades 9–12 dropped out of school in 2012, and poor performance in key subjects at critical points in their education place many others at risk.
>
> Poor health can also act as a barrier to education, particularly when chronic childhood illnesses like asthma and mental health challenges go untreated.
>
> African Americans are more likely to experience chronic disease, violence and injury, emergency mental health treatment and hospitalization, sexually transmitted disease, adverse pregnancy and birth-related outcomes, and risk factors for disease like obesity and high blood pressure. The lack of resources and amenities in neighborhoods where many African Americans live also makes it more difficult to engage in healthy lifestyle behaviors like physical activity and eating a healthy diet.

The almost literal death sentence I felt growing up in North City was not my imagination; it was not me playing the victim but was a harsh reality, an obstacle that I committed to overcome for my family, my community, and myself. This reality was like a wall or a system that spanned health, economics, education, and politics, which worked against me. Even after surmounting these barriers, their presence and the system's pervasive influence persist, subtly reminding me of the hurdles I've overcome.

> *The almost literal death sentence I felt growing up in North City was not my imagination; it was not me playing the victim but was a harsh reality, an obstacle that I committed to overcome for my family, my community, and myself.*

My story reminds me of the power of the human spirit; that if I did it—whatever it is—you can do it, too. Facing insurmountable odds can indeed catalyze greatness and beauty. The experience of being an underdog can transform us in profound and far-reaching ways, and it can open doors to opportunities, impart wisdom, and illuminate paths that once seemed inconceivable.

This narrative isn't just my story; it's a testament to the power of perseverance, the importance of choosing a different path, and the recognition that our stories and leadership are inextricably linked to our history and the communities with which we deeply connect. It's about acknowledging that, against all odds, achieving the unthinkable is within our grasp.

FATHERLESS CHILD

I was conceived one night through the vessels of lust
pain fills my veins
not knowing the past
the future is blind
I cannot see through the fog and rain

If I could face the days before and shed some light on life
I surely would, to put all the confusing thoughts behind
I am quite distant in my heart
from those who think they know me
my life has reached a void
I do feel rather lonely

Is it wrong for me to want to meet
the one who gave me life
and finally get a response to all the questions in my mind

Could I be as scholars label
a disadvantaged child
because my mother is deceased and my father is not around

Often times I prayed that I could have my family back as one
but as I age I realize that what's in the past is done

I am quickly approaching manhood
for all that's good or bad
for all the hell I experienced as child
I solely blame my dad

But being the type of person that I am
Caring, understanding, and forgiving

I will let the pain and hurt recede
and I'll just keep on living
Some say that this is a cycle but believe me it ends here
I'll be there for my child
He will never live in fear

CHAPTER 2

*"Love is an endless act of forgiveness.
Forgiveness is me giving up the right to hurt you for hurting me."*

—Beyoncé

There were four of us. My brother Antwon, affectionately known as Mony, was eighteen months my senior; my younger brother, Cornelius, whom we called NeNe, was eighteen months behind me; and our sister, Carmen, known as Niecy—a nickname inspired by an estranged aunt—was a few years younger than NeNe. As very young kids, we were close, and Mony took on the protector role. One time, someone broke into our apartment to steal some money. Apparently, Mom owed a debt and had been talking freely in the neighborhood about a check she'd received. As the man forcibly came through the shabby wooden door—in front of which we'd placed furniture to keep it closed—Mony, who was eight or nine at the time, inserted himself between the intruder and our tiny shotgun apartment and screamed, "I am going to fuck you up!"

The man slapped him, pushed past his scrawny frame, and then mine as I went to help my brother protect what the man was looking for—the check. After we picked ourselves up from the floor, we knew Mom was going to be pissed off—but Mom was always pissed off.

My little brother was about five, and my sister was barely out of diapers at three. She was like a baby doll, totally incapable of caring for herself. The four of us, one short of a basketball team, typically did everything together. Where one kid went, you generally saw the others. Our mother was gone a lot, so if we were ever allowed to go outside, it was only out front or in the alley. Mom was pretty strict about us sticking close to the apartment, which often meant that our view of outside was through a four-by-four window. We were on the second floor, so if we stuck our bodies out far over the ledge, we could see for what seemed like miles.

The McQueen Apartments, near the intersection of Wabada and Arlington in Saint Louis, epitomized the very essence of neglected housing. Our landlord, Mr. McQueen, whom we saw with predictable regularity once a month, was a classic example of a slumlord. He came to collect rent or engage in other forms of exploitative transactions that kept us tethered to these deteriorating living spaces. The apartments were plagued with a litany of issues: flaking lead-based paint, corroded water faucets, rampant infestations of rats and roaches, and unreliable electrical and plumbing systems were among the most egregious problems we faced daily. I recall Mom mentioning that Mr. McQueen owned many properties in North City, which was decaying fast during this period. In the apartments where we lived and the single-family homes nearby, there were always many women and children.

During summers and weekends, we often had rock fights with kids from the other buildings, where we hurled stones at each other. I remember being hit by a rock on my foot (or maybe it was a broomstick) while running between the floors

31

during one of these battles. The bottom of my left foot was split open, and I bled like a stuck pig.

We met in the alley to fight kids from the other building. You wanted to prove you were no punk. "Yo mama" was enough to ignite passion in my neighborhood and schools. When I think about it today, it's senseless and silly, but back then, it was completely justified to put hands on someone who simply said, "Yo mama." We didn't wait for the additional offense; we circled each other and sized each other up, pointing fingers and hurling insults in the other person's direction. If we really wanted to set them off, we'd push the other person's head as violently as we could with an *index finger* before swinging fists.

At night, on occasion, when there was food, we ate and played with some of the kids in our apartment building. My favorite was salmon croquettes, spaghetti, and fried chicken! We played "Catch a Girl, Get a Girl" and "House" in the alley and in the pile of dirty clothes that filled one room from floor to ceiling. Both "Catch a Girl, Get a Girl" and "House" were highly sexualized games where we mimicked what adults did in the dark, except we kept our clothes on when we humped.

During this period, my mom was consumed by drugs and alcohol. I remember going down to the second floor and pushing the privacy rag out of the hole where the lock had once been. Mom was in the company of several addicts, two men and one other woman, and she had a rope tied around her arm with a needle in it. She seemed barely conscious. I was afraid, but I stood as still as I could so I wouldn't be seen or heard.

I later learned that Mom had a problem with drugs called uppers and downers. Uppers are known for their mentally and physically stimulating effects, and they provide a temporary boost in alertness, energy, and mood. However, when the drug's effects have worn off, the person is left exhausted and depressed. Mom's commonly used uppers included meth and cocaine. On the other hand, downers, which were the opposite of uppers, have a suppressant nature. Drugs like heroin, morphine, fentanyl, and other powerful pain medications fall under this category. They induce feelings of pleasure and relaxation—similar to uppers—by controlling dopamine production with similar side effects. Extended use of opiates leads to unshakable apathy and depression in those who abuse them—something I observed in Mom.

Because my mother stayed up late, we often followed suit. Even when she'd say, "Get your ass in bed," there were only three rooms in our apartment: the front room, a kitchen area, and a sleeping space. Mom slept in the front by the kitchen. I don't recall any doors separating the rooms; curtains prevented us from peering into the front room, yet we could hear everything. Lively discussions filled the air. Mom referred to this apartment as a shotgun apartment. When I asked why, she said it was because you could fire a shotgun from one end, and the shot would travel straight through and out the window onto the streets.

"It's a straight shot," she said.

I realized it wasn't just about being able to fire a shot clear through but also about being able to hear and see straight through. Once, I climbed up off the mat and peeked through the curtains to see what seemed like a bunch of men standing in a single-file line like us kids did to collect our breakfast and lunch at school. It was dark, and there were candles lit.

As I peeked out, I heard a whisper, "Terran"—that's what they called me. I thought it was a nickname, but it turns out it's actually my middle name.

"Terran, come here," the voice said. "You're supposed to have your ass in bed."

"I couldn't sleep," I said.

A man with a deep voice said, "Let him get a piece."

I didn't know what I was about to get. I thought it must be food, so I was excited.

Mom whispered back and forth with the man and mumbled, "He's too young." She finally relented and said, "Okay. Stand in line and do what they do."

So, I stood in line; I was third. The room was dark, only lit by candlelight.

"Take your peewee out," the man in front of me said.

"Okay," I said.

"It's your turn, baby. Now, rub some of this grease on your wee wee," Mom said. By this time, I was standing at attention. The man in front of me moved slowly forward. I could clearly see a woman on the couch where Mom slept. She wasn't moving. The man in front moved forward, and as if straightening me up, Mom firmly took control of my torso and pointed me in his direction because I kept turning around. I couldn't keep still because it was taking too long.

"Now, watch what he does, and you are going to do that," Mom said.

The man put his private part in hers, and after a while, he grunted loudly. My turn was next. I approached the woman. She smelled like garbage—like the garbage in our alley after it sat for two weeks. I did what Mom told me; I inserted my wee wee the same as the man in front of me and humped. The feeling reminded me of "Catch a Girl, Get a Girl," but this was more intense. *Wow*, I thought, *this is amazing!*

I kept humping, not sure what the outcome would be, until Mom said, "That's enough."

"But I didn't grunt, Mom," I said.

"Next!" she said.

As I caught my breath and began to stumble away, she said, "Put your hands out."

I did, and she poured some terrible smelling liquid into my cupped hands.

"This is rubbing alcohol. Rub it on your wee wee." I did, not knowing what it was for.

The man on the side, smiling in my direction, said. "It will stop rashes. You're a man now."

What's a rash? I thought.

I retreated to the corner, exhilarated by what I had just encountered. When the last man finished humping, Mom poured some rubbing alcohol on the woman's private area, lit a cigarette, and put the cigarette in the woman's hand, then placed the woman's hand with the lit cigarette on the woman's private area. I saw fire and then heard a scream. I was terrified. *What is happening?* I thought.

The woman jumped up, and Mom said, "Bitch you fell asleep with a cigarette in your hand."

The woman somehow found her way out of the dark apartment and into the streets. I could hear her screams get fainter and fainter until I didn't hear them anymore. I don't know what this woman did to my mother, but I never saw her again.

MY MOTHER AND THE PEOPLE she ran with didn't get up and go to work. I never saw them engage in purposeful activity, which underscored that an idle mind is the devil's workshop. Without positive examples, I was on the slippery slope of taking things whenever the opportunity arose, just like everyone else I knew.

Whether school was in session or not, most days consisted of sleeping in and getting up late. So, I missed a lot of school. I stayed home with my siblings and listened to the women gossip about their soap operas. The women in our apartment complex lived by their stories—*As the World Turns, Guiding Light, All My Children*—blared throughout. We would mark the passage of time by what soap or television show like *The Price is Right* was on. *Guiding Light* was a favorite of my mom's, and over the years, I also came to appreciate the drama, though I spent most of my days not watching soaps but watching my younger brother and sister and trying to find something to eat.

I had a lot of anxiety that we wouldn't get enough food to eat, and we often didn't.

I had a lot of anxiety that we wouldn't get enough food to eat, and we often didn't. We tried to make do with what we had. The government feeding program sometimes would give us bread, canned braunschweiger meat, cheese, powdered milk, and powdered eggs. This was good eating. When those items ran out, we could have sugar sandwiches if we had bread and sugar. Bread, mustard, mayonnaise, or just about any spread on bread would temporarily satisfy our hunger.

My brother got good at serving up fried cornmeal mush, which was cornmeal stirred with water and then deep fried. Mom often disappeared for hours and days at a time, leaving us to fend for ourselves. I never quite understood why she was so angry when she returned home and learned that we'd been cooking. Once, just after my brother had fried up his cornmeal mush, we heard Mom coming up the steps. My brother rushed over to the window and hurled the food out the window. I was so hungry I could have followed that food out the two-story window.

Mom came in and said, "What the fuck are you doing?"

"Nothing," we said in harmony.

"You are doing something; I can smell it," she said. I never got the courage to ask Mom why she was so mad.

It certainly couldn't have been that she was angry because we were little and cooking with an electric skillet, seeing that, at times, we heated the apartment with the oven. We typically ate the best for about a week at the beginning of every month when welfare checks arrived. The food stamps or government food never lasted as long as we'd hoped. We got used to the hunger, but we never liked it.

I HAD AN IMAGINATION as a kid. I loved *Superman* and *CHIPs*, a crime drama. I pretended I was a cop and was strong like Erik Estrada, "Ponch," as he was called, and I had the powers of Superman. Superman didn't have to worry about food. As a young boy, during one of those days that I didn't go to school, I broke into my neighbor's apartment to steal food. I wondered what Ponch or Superman would have thought about that decision, but I was desperate. In my idleness, I saw an opportunity and took it. For every choice, there's a consequence. But when you're living a hard life, you aren't worried about the consequences. To survive, you do desperate things, like waiting

My oldest brother and I would often go scavenging through the dumpster to find food.

for the local school cafeteria workers to throw away expired food. In my mind, food never expired.

My oldest brother and I often scavenged through the dumpster to find food. Sometimes, the items were nicely bundled.

"Look," I would say, "all of that food is in the milkcrate!"

I've often wondered if that was a coincidence or if we were expected guests. To secure food, I often begged the lunch lady for two meals and begged my classmates for their free breakfast and lunch tickets before and after school. They often looked at me as if I was pitiful, but I didn't care. I was hungry.

Sometimes, we would get lucky in the alley behind our apartment.

"Look, Mony," I said in amazement. "There's some fried chicken that's only been half eaten, and look at these clothes!"

The clothes included underwear, jeans, and shirts that were about our sizes.

"We only need to swat away the bees and flies and separate out the food that has maggots on it," I said.

We had what turned out to be a great meal. The clothes also seemed perfectly fine to wear as is.

I wasn't particularly interested in school. The only reason I went to school was to eat and feel safe. When I went to school, I liked to get there early to ensure I ate breakfast.

However, I was very competitive with certain aspects of school. For example, I found great joy in memorizing my times tables. We would sometimes have competitions to see who could go from 1 x 1 = 1 to 12 x 12 = "I'm not sure!" I loved the energy this created. Even though I didn't practice enough to ever be that good at it, I still enjoyed it.

My favorite subjects were recess, lunch, and the end of school. I loved playing kickball during recess. I was pretty good at kicking the big red ball far and throwing the ball hard enough to tag other kids out. I generally aimed for their heads if the teachers weren't looking. We also played dodgeball; I loved being the last man standing. During lunch, I made it a point to try to get full because I wasn't sure when I would eat again. When the end-of-day school bell rang, I always jumped out of my seat in a rush to get out of class first, pushing past other kids, only to be scolded by the teacher to "Sit down."

I hated sitting in class—my mind was typically on the stuff that wasn't being taught. Throughout grade school and somewhat into high school, I was labeled "special," mostly because I had difficulty learning—probably because I barely attended school. When I attended, I craved attention in any way I could get it, including being disruptive in class, picking fights, and always running hot. I never backed down from a fight.

Once, I spit gum in a White girl's finely textured hair to see what would happen. I knew if someone spit gum into my hair, I would whip their ass, so it never happened to me. But if it had, the gum would hit my tightly wound curls and drop to the floor. *But she has stringy hair,* I thought all through class—it was my preoccupation. She sat right in front of me so the gum didn't have to go far from my juicy lips. I ensured the gum was nice and wet before I drew a deep breath and blew as if blowing out stubborn birthday candles.

The gum landed in her hair, and she screamed, "Why did you do that?" and looked back at me with a scowl.

All eyes were now on me. I slouched in my seat and said, "Do what?" trying to deflect attention.

The more she tried to untangle the gum, the more "oohs" I heard from the class. I saw trouble coming my way. I was sent to the principal's office and got suspended. I really didn't have a reason to do that other than the attention I got being a nuisance to my classmate. I guess I was just *special.* Being special typically meant that I attended some smaller classes and spent more time talking to counselors, designated mentors, therapists, and the principal when I went to school. I certainly had an imagination.

I was also fascinated with learning to write in cursive. Cursive writing was like a foreign language. We had white tracing cardboard that we could take home to perfect our cursive writing. Being left-handed, I was always frustrated because my writing always smeared across the page, as if I had wiped mud on the page. It also left a black stain from the lead pencil on the side of my hand. *Eh,* I thought, as I spit on my hand and wiped back and forth on my pants to clean it, *I should have been right-handed.* The school desks were for right-handed kids only, and I had to sit awkwardly, twisting my body to write.

I would have been right-handed, but once, I was crawling behind my older brother in one of our apartments. He didn't see me when he went into the bathroom. I was crossing the threshold behind him as quickly as I could crawl. He pushed the door, which was three times his size, shut. My mom said that I screamed so loud that she "About had a heart attack."

They couldn't save my right pinky finger despite their efforts. After that, Mom started putting things in my left hand to make that my dominant hand. Kids teased me all through childhood, saying, "You crippled" and calling me "four finger boy" and "nine and a half." I would lash right back at them. With each taunt, I grew angrier and angrier. So, I would just fight and get suspended. It seems like I was always out of school, but I didn't care because I could escape by watching the powerful Victor Newman of *The Young and the Restless*, who never let anyone push him around. While Victor stood his ground on TV, I found a sense of strength and solace from my own battles.

My mother was a tall, busty, big-boned woman. She had caramel skin and, from what I can recall, big *brownish* hair—the kind of hair women sported on the 1970s TV show *Soul Train*. She seemed to be struggling with her value and worth, as evidenced by the string of men, drug-induced comas, and persistent disappearance for hours (if not days) on end when she left us kids unprotected.

Her name was Carolyn. She was an only child with no significant or deep family connections. I have vague memories of visiting cousins, but not to a frequency that would make it normal. There were several men in and out of Mom's life, and she mainstreamed them into our lives by telling us they were our "uncles." Our uncles occasionally brought us food, and most smelled like the vent from a fast-food dive—like they'd doused themselves with fryer oil.

Of these men, the one who seemed to go away and come back more than any of them was Ulysses. We called him US. US was seemingly the father of my oldest brother and stood no more than five foot five in stature. US had an explosive temper. While I have fragments of memories, they weren't pleasant. Mom and US argued and fought a lot, usually about, "Who are you fucking?" They exchanged blows in jealous outbursts on many occasions. They also lashed out viciously at others who came in between their unstable relationship.

On one occasion, US returned home after a stint presumably in jail and beat one of mom's boyfriends with a baseball bat and dragged him down the back staircase of our multi-story redbrick apartment complex in the city. Apparently, this boyfriend had slapped or pushed my oldest brother. The ambulance was called to cart him away, and US was once more on the run for assault. US ended up going to prison for a very long time after he robbed some business. I think it was a local grocery store.

ANOTHER UNCLE. When I was five, my mom started bringing a man named Curtis Jr. to the house. He was a stranger to me, but my mom said he was my uncle—Uncle Curtis. Uncle Curtis would show up at our home periodically and hang out with Mom and his brother, who was the father of my two younger siblings. Mom, Uncle Curtis, and his brother would sometimes drink and have what seemed like a good time together. One summer, he started coming around more often because "we were a handful," as Mom would say. My three other siblings ranged in age from one to seven years. Uncle Curtis would sometimes sleep over in the area where we kids slept. There was always a lot of hugging and lap-sitting.

"Come here," he would say, pointing in my direction.

Mom didn't have to tell us to be polite. "I'll whoop they ass if they don't mind me," she often said. I didn't want my ass whooped, so I "mined" adults. This meant "do what you are told."

I started finding myself alone with Uncle Curtis. I hated it when he came over. He would make me touch his private area, controlling my hand and head to rub him back and forth until he released himself. He forced himself so far into my mouth that I would choke and vomit. He was angry as he violently assaulted my young body. I somehow knew it was wrong, in a way only a five-year-old could. To endure, I stopped feeling. I stopped thinking, overwhelmed by the situation. I stopped being able to preserve my life. The experience was beyond comprehension. *What had I done to deserve this?* I'd wonder immediately afterward as I escaped the bathroom and hovered in a corner of a room. I couldn't comprehend what was happening. I felt fear every day, whether he was around or not.

This abusive behavior escalated quickly. One day, Uncle Curtis was at the house, and Mom said she was going to take the three other kids to the park and leave me in his care. I became very frightened and visibly shaken.

I grabbed my mom's leg and begged, "Momma, don't leave me."

She pulled me off her leg and asked, "Boy, what is wrong with you?"

I didn't have the words, and because I was in the company of Uncle Curtis, I definitely didn't want to say it out loud. Uncle Curtis always swore that if I ever told anyone what he was doing to me, "I will kill you, your brothers, and your sister." I believed him.

I finally gathered the courage to tell Mom that Uncle Curtis was touching me and forcing me to touch him with my hands and mouth on his front and back. I couldn't think of any other words to describe what was happening.

She said, "What do you mean? What is he doing exactly?" Enough tears streamed to put out a fire, and shaking on the inside and almost paralyzed on the outside, I shared what had become my fiery hell. I knew that Uncle Curtis was going to

TWICE OVER A MAN

kill me, but I didn't care. I would rather be dead than be left alone with him.

Mom stood stunned for what seemed like forever. She then went into her room and walked out with a heightened level of intensity and a shotgun shouting, "I am going to kill you, you son of a bitch!"

I wanted her to kill him. But there was another adult in the house; it had to be Curtis Jr.'s brother. He talked her out of killing Curtis, and she called the police instead.

When they arrived and heard the story, I faintly remember an officer saying, "Why didn't you shoot him?" Curtis was arrested. I wanted her to kill him.

Mom told me, "Baby, you're going to have to testify in court." I didn't know what *testify* or *court* meant, but over the course of some time, I remember talking to several White people and being even more afraid.

One day, I showed up at the courthouse, and a kind White lady said, "Once you tell the truth about what happened to you, we are going to give you some money."

That made me happy and gave me the energy to press on. I was always hungry; we needed the money. It was then that I learned words like *molestation* and *rape*. I shared as much as I could and answered a lot of questions, and I remember getting some money in a small manila envelope. Later, Mom said that Curtis Jr. was going to be in jail for a long time and that I would be safe.

From that point, everything changed for me. During my early years, I encountered and witnessed sexual abuse and sexual assault, the residue of which became a stronghold that attempted to arrest my development. I couldn't escape the smells that triggered me. I couldn't escape my thoughts, whether asleep or awake; I couldn't reconcile the pain. Despite my mother's assurance that "you will be safe," safety remained elusive to me.

43

My mother once told me, "You are a mistake, and I don't love you."

I felt like it was the alcohol and drugs speaking and not my mother; nonetheless, it left me feeling like I was naked and like anyone could see and do anything to me, that there was no one to care for me. *Maybe I am a mistake*, I thought. Not having anyone to care for me made me harder. Not having anyone to care for me made me bitter. I was easily enraged and always wanted to fight, but my relationship with my mother was short lived.

One morning, I woke up early—and very hungry. I climbed up from the floor where I slept and made my way to the kitchen to see what there was to eat. I only found a box of saltine crackers in the refrigerator. We typically kept food that belonged in the pantry in the refrigerator to guard against roaches and mice. The roaches would scatter when we turned the lights on, but the mice didn't move when we opened the bin at the bottom of the fridge where we kept potatoes when we had them. They were always there falling over themselves; it was disgusting.

By this time, any aid we got from the state went straight into my mom's veins. She'd become a chronic drug user. She woke up using, and she fell asleep using, a rubber wire tied around her left arm while her right hand injected her worries away. So, I wasn't surprised when I left the kitchen and found her sleeping in the living room. I wanted to ask her if I could eat some crackers—we had to ask to eat because food was hard to come by. When she didn't respond, I began shaking her.

"Momma, Momma, wake up!"

She still didn't respond. I continued to shake her, and again, there was no response. By this time, my two brothers and sister had woken up. We knew something was wrong. My mom's face looked almost blue. Because we didn't have a telephone, I hurried to the back of our shotgun apartment, kicked up the four-by-four that was wedged against the door and the wall to keep it locked (because we had no lock), and rushed across the gangway to the neighbor's apartment. I was banging violently on her door when she answered.

I screamed, "Something is wrong with Momma!"

"Huh?" she replied.

I yelled once more, "Something is wrong! She's not moving!"

Our neighbor called 911 and explained that we needed help and lived in the apartments on the corner of Wabada and Arlington, on the top floor. Despite all the noise and commotion, Mom didn't move.

Finally, the paramedics arrived. "What happened?" they bellowed.

"We aren't sure," I said. "She normally wakes up. Her face is a different color from the other times," I said.

The paramedics tried to bring my mom back to life, but they couldn't. As we watched nervously, huddled together within feet of her eerily still body, they pronounced her dead. She was twenty-eight years old.

We were sad for Mom. And we were sad for ourselves, not knowing where we were going to live or if we would ever live together again. It was a very difficult moment to comprehend. I don't think we understood the finality of death, and we had no real concept of family beyond the four of us. The police asked a lot of questions about our "next of kin." We didn't have anyone that we could remember. Before the police arrived, we had concocted a scheme to say that our next-door neighbor was our aunt. I

The paramedics tried to bring my mom back to life, but they couldn't. As we watched nervously . . . they pronounced her dead in our apartment. She was twenty-eight years old.

don't recall why, but that lie fell apart quickly. Then, a light bulb came on! We remembered a cousin who lived on the next street over—on Semple Avenue. Mom had taken us over there a couple of times.

We hopped into the police cruiser, and in a matter of minutes, we pulled up in front of a large yellow and green home located in the 2800 block of Semple. On that day, we became parentless wards of the state. Frozen in the moment, I often found myself staring into space, thinking about my mom, not wanting to believe she was gone for good. It was overwhelming.

Over the ensuing days, my emotions were a chaotic whirl-wind, firing in all directions. I was happy at the prospect of eating when I was hungry, but I was mostly sad, angry, and disappointed. I was depressed and filled with anxiety. I was so angry and disappointed in her—for killing herself with drugs, for what she had allowed Uncle Curtis to do to me, for not fighting harder to overcome what I now know as oppressive poverty, and for our hunger.

My mom died in August of 1982 when I was about to start third grade. Within weeks of her death, I found out that I would be held back in school.

"What does this mean?" I cried.

"It means you won't go to third grade with the rest of your class."

I was so embarrassed. Not only had I lost Mom, but I lost all my friends because I was a special stupid kid.

Mom's death and being held back that year forced me to realize that not every relationship is lifelong, including those with family and friends. It also taught me that some of the things we get in life are things we deserve—like being held back—and some things we don't deserve, like Mom dying without reconciling her love back to me.

DISTANCE

As I transcend those days of the past
And try to make some sense of it all
I covertly construct territorial bounds
And create distance with obscure walls
Each emotion I feel is distinguished in this sense
It's reflective of my childhood and all the love that I missed
A mother's love for her child
And a father's love for his son
Is the ultimate in adoration
But I experienced neither one
As we all know a flower without water is surely destined to die
It's easy to see why a child without love would feel the need
to cry
In an effort to strike harmony and balance within my life
I suppress the mental residue of dysfunctional family ties
I take journeys of great distance
As individual as it may seem
Physically I am at a standstill,
But only I control my dreams

CHAPTER 3

"If you're going through hell, keep going."
—*Winston Churchill*

Riding in the police cruiser, making our way down the steep hill on Semple, I noticed mostly single-family homes and only a few big buildings like the one I lived in with Mom. As we pointed out the house to the police officer, he immediately pulled over. From the street, the yellow and green frame house in the 2800 block towered over us. It looked like a mansion, and for a moment, I thought, *Everything is going to be OK.* We walked up to the screen door, which hung from its hinges in front of the closed front door. After the officer knocked, a woman's eyeball peered at us through the peephole in the door. It swung open.

I didn't know that I was about to enter Missouri's foster care system. I didn't know the system would be my "home" for ten years or more. I didn't know that we were four of about 13,000 kids in foster care in Missouri in 1982, part of a nationwide community of about 600,000 kids who are wards of the state. I didn't know that the State of Missouri now had legal custody over me—with ultimate control over who would parent me. I didn't know that a government agency, the Division of Family Services, was now responsible for keeping me safe. And I didn't know that my appearance before a judge in the Curtis Jr. case would become the first of many court and child welfare appearances for this young boy.

I didn't know that I was about to enter Missouri's foster care system.

In Missouri, as in most states, the foster care system recognizes three types of placement: group homes, community homes, and kinship care, where you stay with a family member. The state prefers kinship care because it reasons that such care will maintain important family connections. After all, who is more likely to take good care of a defenseless child—a relative or a stranger?

The woman who belonged to the eyeball in the door was a relative, but she was a stranger to me. I would learn later that she was Shirley, my mom's third cousin, the one we'd come looking for. As she swung the door open, I encountered a massive human form with huge hands and unbelievably large earlobes. Past her imposing thighs was an entryway large enough to double as a sitting room. An elderly woman sat in a stained orange recliner.

The living room was directly to the right of the entry. It had a large wooden cabinet-style television. Family photos, someone's family, anyway—it sure didn't feel like mine—hung on the wall and lined the floor, resting against the vintage brown television/record player combo. I remember a sofa and two recliners in the living room. I guessed that at least one of the recliners belonged to the woman standing in front of me.

A staircase ascended to the second floor to the left of the entry door. I could see the first few steps and a small, dimly lit landing before it turned and disappeared behind the wall. About twenty steps directly in front of the entrance was a small kitchen near the back of the house. As I entered, I could see a small table, a refrigerator, and an upright deep freezer with a lock on it. I wondered why the deep freezer had a lock on it.

To the right of the kitchen was a formal dining room turned into a bedroom that had a stench that hit me before I crossed the threshold to enter the room. The smell was from a bedside toilet in the carpeted room. This bedroom was adjacent to a storage room that had once been a hair salon. Now, it was a remnant of its former self with an old top-loading porcelain washer that had seen better days piled high with a bunch of junk. I would become intimately familiar with that washer because I was told to hold onto it and not let go while being beaten across my backside in the coming years.

On the second floor, there was a larger landing and hall, and Shirley's bedroom was at the back of the house. There was also a bathroom and a second and third bedroom, both of which were padlocked until special guests arrived.

Within days after the police had left and we were as settled in as we could be, I stood at the top of the staircase in the shadows and heard my mom's aunt and uncle from Chicago talk to Shirley about what they should do with all of us. I didn't know these people, either, and I was really confused by all the heated back and forth.

"How much is the state paying for these kids?" I heard.

Another voice said, "It's not enough."

I shouted down, "I don't want to go with you anyway." I didn't know who I was talking to, and Shirley issued a shush.

"Stay out of grown folks' business," she called up the stairs. Those people left, and we only saw them once or twice more when we were a little older.

SHIRLEY DIDN'T HAVE ANY CHILDREN of her own. Being a parent would be all new to her, but she did have a lot of nieces and nephews.

Pete and Rowena, the daughters of Jimmy (Shirley's sister), were her favorites. They were young adults. When Pete came home, presumably from college, he stayed in one of the special padlocked rooms on the second floor when he wasn't bunking on the couch on the first floor.

Rowena had three children. She lived up the street at the beginning of the block, closer to where we lived when Mom died. Shirley affectionately called Rowena's kids "the girls"—Shauntay, Brandy, and Shalonda.

Shirley had two sisters, Frieda and Brenda. Frieda also lived in North City and seemed well educated and wealthier—I think she was a schoolteacher. She had a son, Tony, who was in the military. Her sister, Brenda, lived near Columbia, Missouri, with her husband, Charles, and their two children, Deanna and Russ. Russ was about the age of my older brother, and Deanna was about my younger sister's age. They were nice, uninhibited kids—which was very different from the shyness we displayed to survive. Russ always wore the newest popular shoes and clothes. I wanted to be like them.

She also had two brothers, Ralph and Johnny. Ralph was a dark-skinned man who worked at a local utility company—probably a lineman, judging by how he dressed. He was very attentive to his mother. He was married to Regina, who was as yellow as the sun and had an energy that reminded me of sunshine. She was outgoing and would always say, "Come here and give me a hug."

Ralph and Regina had two children, Brian and Jason, who were a little older than we were. They came by the house almost every Sunday to bring a plate of food to Ora—the old lady Shirley cared for.

Shirley's other brother, Johnny, lived out of the country and would occasionally visit with his wife, whom he presumably married while serving a tour in Vietnam. The family was so proud of him. Pictures of him in his military uniform were prominently displayed on the wall leading up the staircase. When Johnny and his wife visited, I don't remember them ever really talking to us, but they would stay at least six weeks every year.

Her cousin, old man Willie, lived in the basement. Willie always had a pocket full of change, and he would get up every day, put on a suit, and catch the bus downtown to hang out. The old woman in the recliner was my Great Aunt Ora, my great-grandmother's sister. Shirley had once operated a beauty salon out of an add-on room off the back of the house where the old washer was, but caring for Ora was now Shirley's primary responsibility.

But I was more than a poor foster kid; I was a poor Black foster kid. I had nothing.

Then, we showed up.

FEAR AND LONELINESS. These were my constant companions as a kid. My brothers, sister, and I were on an island within the family. We were the outcasts, second-class citizens among the nieces and nephews. That island was about survival. However, I was alone on an island within that island because, for whatever reason, Shirley treated me the worst. It was a very lonely place, and that loneliness has stayed with me my entire life. I felt abandoned; I was in it alone. As my life in foster care continued, I learned that foster kids are a different, lower class of poor kids. If you're poor, you at least have a family looking after you. But I was more than a poor foster kid; I was a poor Black foster kid. I had nothing. I was in a family, but I was not of a family.

My fear of Shirley was unlike any fear I have felt since. The silence from everyone who visited that house only reinforced that I'd been silenced, too—I had no voice, and the rules that normal society lived by didn't apply to me. It was terrifying. When I grew older, that fear would become vaguer but more debilitating as it affected my mind, impeded my actions, and twisted my faith. It became the foundation on which my life was built as I lay awake at night thinking about my mother, my father, all the mistakes they'd made, and wondered if my life was destined to be the same, laden with unfulfilled potential and mismanaged gifts.

When the nieces and nephews came to visit, it was like magic. Shirley loved those kids, especially Deanna, Russ, and "the girls." She would smile and laugh as the nieces and nephews ran in and out of the house and played in the yard. Their presence was palpable. She became lighter for those hours and days, and the whole house seemed to lift with her. But when they left, the magic left with them, and the house became heavy again—heavy with Shirley and the burden of being forced to care for us, the unexpected, the unloved, and the unwanted.

The contrast between how Shirley felt about her other relatives and how she felt about us was painful. Literally. It soon became clear that she had organized the house into a perverse geography of pain. The first floor was for aggressive and violent shakes and attacks. The landing on the stairs was for sitting alone when we had been "bad," the TV impossible to see but impossible not to hear from the ledge in the other room. I put my imagination to work creating images to go with the sounds for shows like *The Cosby Show*. When Pete and Brenda weren't there, their bedrooms on the second floor were used to store gifts Shirley had accumulated over the years and for, as she would say, "beating the hell out of us." Nothing was worse than the bathroom.

"Strip and get your ass in that tub," she said as she drew water into the tub.

As soon as the water filled to my stomach, she'd come in with an extension cord. There was no place to hide as she violently swung the cord, welting my entire body as I sloshed around the water, trying to find refuge. There was none to be found.

Mom had occasionally become overwhelmed and frustrated with us and beat us, but it was nothing like how Shirley beat us, especially me. I never thought of Mom's beatings as abusive; when I think about my mom, the feelings are more about chronic hunger, abandonment, and neglect because of Curtis Jr. than malice.

Shirley had malice; she struck fear in me. She seemed to always be getting ready to beat us or recovering after beating us, so she could beat us again. It was premeditated, and she just had too much on her. She would use those big hands to slap the sides of my face at the same time with all the force she could muster, like she was flattening a hamburger, leaving my ears ringing. If not clinging to the old washer on the first floor, she would make me strip naked in Pete and Brenda's room and lie on the bed so she could beat me with a thick leather belt. It had a huge, shiny metal buckle like I'd never seen before or since. It was painful. Each blow was like a little bit of death. Trying to get up during those beatings was impossible.

I'd get hit once, jump up instinctively, and Shirley would yell, "Get your ass down before I kill you!"

One time, my face was bashed in so badly that it felt like what I imagined getting kicked in the face by a bull would feel like. On that day, I was sure she was going to kill me, and I was OK with that.

"GET YOUR ASS OVER HERE!" she screamed. I walked slowly into Brenda's room. "Lay across that fucking bed," she yelled.

My body didn't even hit the mattress before the onslaught. I cried and begged, "Please, please, no more!"

Unable to get many words out between the strikes, I scurried across the bed to the other side so she couldn't reach me.

She let the slack out of the belt and screamed, "Get your ass back over here. I am going to kill you, motherfucker."

She swung the belt buckle and struck me on my chest. My body shook like the ground during an earthquake, and before I could see it coming, the belt buckle smashed me in the face. I fell to the floor as she came around the bed, still swinging the belt. I just lay there. I had no more fight in me.

She didn't kill me, but she killed my will to live.

My chest was busted open and bleeding. I could sense the sorrow from my siblings. My mouth swelled up larger than a deformed baseball. I couldn't eat or speak well, drooling each time I opened my mouth. Shirley wouldn't take me to the doctor; instead, in a moment of compassion, she gave me a sock filled with ice.

I nursed my wounds with that sock and ice. When Sunday came around, Ralph and Sunshine walked in. Ralph looked at my face and lashed out at Shirley. But this wasn't the first time we'd been hurt by Shirley. Something about the visibility of my injury didn't sit well with Ralph. They shouted back and forth.

Ralph said, "You are sick! What is this? Why haven't you taken him to the hospital?"

"If you want to take them, you can take them!" Shirley yelled at Ralph.

Shirley's default when challenged was always, "You can take them to live with you if you care so much."

That was the problem. No one cared—not Ralph or anyone else in the family wanted anything to do with us permanently broken kids.

My mouth was messed up for a while after that, and it was swollen shut for about a week. As the scar tissue began to form, so did my aversion to mirrors and posing for pictures. From that point forward, I hated looking at my reflection, and I couldn't wait to grow facial hair, thinking I could mask the scar. I always wanted to sit on the passenger side of the school bus closest to the window so I'd be the only one who could see Shirley's scar reflected back. Even as an adult, I've found myself favoring certain seats and positions in photos. It was all tied to that day, though that day was just one of many.

The abuse happened almost daily, and usually for no reason that was logical. Something just triggered her. As a result, my brothers and sister and I fought with each other as a coping mechanism, like prisoners will. We tried to stay on Shirley's good side, which often meant ensuring that someone else was on her bad side.

When Shirley returned home from church or an Order of Eastern Stars meeting, we kids rushed down the steps or bolted full steam from the kitchen—or wherever Ora had us sit to keep us separated and avoid "messing" with each other. As soon as I heard the muffler of Shirley's car, a sense of dread came over me—every time. The car door would shut, and within a matter of seconds, the screen door would open, then the lock on the door would turn. Conditioned to do so, we would rush to the door as it opened and tattle on the others.

The abuse happened almost daily, and usually for no reason that was logical.

"Shirley, Antwon hit me," or "Orvin said a bad word," or whatever it was. We wanted to be on her good side. We all knew that someone was getting beat no matter what.

Ora would scream, "Shut up. Shut it up." Lifting her frail arm and pointing, Ora would single out who she felt was at fault for the misdemeanor offenses that brought about capital punishment. And we deserved it, as Ora would often say, "You bad ass kids."

Except for rare instances, like the day Ralph—infuriated—spoke up, or the time an anonymous neighbor hotlined Shirley (I suspected it was the woman who lived right next door, who often witnessed us being snatched violently into the house), no one else who visited the house did anything to acknowledge or stop the beatings. Our feeling of isolation grew and contributed to the weird, dysfunctional group we'd created among ourselves. Shirley ruled by fear, and we weren't the only ones in her grip.

The abuse unfolded in the open and was a stark contrast to the care Shirley showed Ora. As Ora's strength waned under the burden of age and daily dialysis, she became more of a silent witness instead of a facilitator, sitting in her recliner and drifting in and out of consciousness as her days passed with the flicker of TV shows and the backdrop of Cardinals games on KMOX. Those broadcasts became the soundtrack to my languishing days, punctuated only by Shirley's outbursts of cruelty—her own twisted version of hitting a home run. Each moment of seeming excitement for her was a moment of suffering for me.

SHIRLEY SEEMED TO LIKE my youngest brother the best, and I resented him for it. Most of the time, all four of us kids slept in the hallway on two mattresses on the second floor. The three boys packed in the full-sized bed, two on one end, with the person in the middle on the opposite end to create space. One night, I fell asleep and dreamed I was using the bathroom, only to wake up and realize I'd wet the bed. Afraid and trying to think of a way out of the beating, I looked over at my younger brother and thought, *Shirley really likes him.* So, I decided to pee on him and say that he had peed on me. That was the plan.

He woke up, yelling, "What are you doing? Are you pissing on me?"

I was caught. In the commotion, everybody woke up, including Shirley. It was about 5:00 a.m., around the time we got up for school anyway. I got a beating for that one and had to sleep standing up all night for the next few days before being upgraded to sleeping while sitting slouched on a milkcrate. These were common forms of punishment and torture.

On the days that I had to stand to sleep, Shirley took the shade off the lamp, placed the lamp behind us, and said, "Don't touch this lamp. Stand your ass right here."

We could see our shadows dancing off her wall when we fidgeted, and could hear her say, between the sounds of whatever she was watching on television, "Stand your ass still."

We learned that the light reflected our shadows, one taller than the other, off the wall in Shirley's room, so she could check on us at any point in the night to ensure we were still standing.

Sometimes, it was my oldest brother and me. We discovered that if one of us stood really close to the light, it would cast a bigger shadow, obscuring the second person so the second one could sleep. We took turns sleeping on the floor. Easing down to the floor was the hardest part because the floors creaked, and we didn't want to wake Shirley. Once when I was on shift, I fell asleep against the wall and slid all the way down to the floor. I woke to the boom of my face planting on the hardwood floor, only to see Shirley and feel her tossing my body like a ragdoll, swinging that belt.

"You had better not wake me again," she yelled at me. "And get your ass up," she yelled at my brother.

When I was "good," she allowed me to sleep while sitting on the milkcrate. This was the same kind of milkcrate that we would cut a hole in the bottom, hang on a tree in the alley, and use as a basketball hoop. Shirley gave me a gray wool-like blanket that was itchy, but it was better than standing all night, though not as good as sleeping flat on the creaky wood floor. I would prop myself up against Pete's padlocked bedroom door and go to sleep. In the morning, my face was smooshed from the door, my back and knees hurt, and I was often so very tired. I developed a wartime condition from this experience where I could fall asleep anywhere on demand.

On the days I slept standing or on the milkcrate, I couldn't wait to get to school to sleep with my head resting comfortably on my arms atop the desk. I couldn't focus, and often the teachers turned a blind eye, as if knowing my home life was complicated.

Memories of those years haunt me. I did my homework at the kitchen table. It was always so tense, especially when doing math. Shirley hovered over me, saying, "You'd better get the right answer."

If I didn't, as evidenced by a simple erasure mark, she slapped my hand with a thick ruler until it was red and shaking. And if I seemed distracted by her presence, she aggressively pushed my head into the books and gestured for me to focus on my work. I couldn't control my nerves, and I trembled as she loomed over me in the background, waiting to slap my hand if I got the wrong answer. It made it hard for me to think and process what was in front of me, and I fidgeted as if I was going to be struck for making any sound, even when she retreated to the other room.

Once, Shirley forced me to eat liver, which I hated. After eating it, I silently threw it up onto my plate. I couldn't help it. Then, Shirley made me eat what I had thrown up and then beat me.

Shirley kept plenty of food in that deep freezer, but she was so strict.

"No seconds," she would say after cooking my favorite, fried chicken.

I swore at that time that I would never have more kids than I could feed well. The deep freezer was padlocked, and she carefully monitored the contents of the refrigerator and pantry. I was once beaten for stealing a piece of chocolate cake, but it was worth it.

One Christmas, I was gifted one of those coin banks that looked like a Tootsie Roll. There were maybe a few dollars of coins in it. It sat at the base of the TV in the living room alongside family pictures. During punishments, I would sit at the bottom of the staircase, looking at Shirley in her recliner, my resentment growing stronger every day. I imagined pushing past her, grabbing the Tootsie Roll bank, running away, and living off the coins.

One day, I told Shirley that I was going to take my Tootsie Roll bank and run away, to which she said, "Take it and get your Black ass out of here," towering over me and gesturing toward the front door. I wasn't brave enough to actually do it, but thinking about it gave me comfort many days. There would be no escaping Shirley.

Eventually, Cousin Willie died, and my brother Antwon and I moved into the basement. The basement would periodically flood, leaving that mildew smell. The toilet smelled of sewer gas, and there was mold, but we didn't mind. Antwon was on one side, and I was on the other—islands unto ourselves, each of us in our own little place. Sometime after that, Shirley was getting ready to beat Antwon, but he was done with it.

An athlete, physically fit and good with his hands, he screamed at her, "If you hit me, I'll fuck you up!"

I took him at his word. My brother wasn't scared of anybody and ran with a rough crowd. Football saved his life by keeping him off the street. Shirley, likely processing all of this, took him at his word, too.

As she turned the corner to walk up the basement steps, she said, "Stand right here, motherfucker. I'll be right back."

We both knew she was going to get the twenty-two-caliber pistol she kept in the house. Antwon didn't stay. He grabbed a few items and left for good.

I HAD REASONS TO BE DEPRESSED. Childhood was complicated. My mother had died at age twenty-eight, and I don't know if I understood this wasn't ordinary. I hadn't seen anyone die up to that point, and without a picture of how old you should be when you die, I began to believe that I wouldn't live past twenty-eight. I had an internal struggle between my desire for life and my desire for death.

With Shirley, I thought often of what the world would be like without me in it. She killed my will to live. Once, I concocted a plan to drown myself in a tub of water. My young mind wasn't developed enough to realize that without a sedative or something that brought about paralysis, I couldn't simply *will* my death in a tub of water. Once submerged, I held my breath as if jumping into the deep end of the pool and going to the bottom, unconsciously counting 1-1,000, 2-1,000, 3-1,000. But my instincts were always to pop back to the surface for air by the time I got to 4-1,000. My instinct was to pop back up for life. I don't know if I actually wanted to kill myself deep down—at least, that's what I told my therapist. When I said that, he embraced me like I imagined being embraced by a father.

"What were you thinking?" he mumbled as I settled into his arms.

"I don't know if I *was* thinking," I whispered.

What I was feeling was pain. That pain has been a constant, and I suppose I really wanted to kill the *pain*, not *myself*.

He told me in that brief moment of peace, "Your life is valuable."

I don't know if I believed him. Other people had said the same thing, only to place me back under Shirley's roof, but it was an optimistic seed.

The football field became a place for me to start working out my feelings more constructively, but one day, I was clipped—hit from the back—and took a bad fall. I was in terrible pain.

"Don't touch me!" I screamed as my teammates tried to lift me up.

I lay in the grassy field, looking up at the stars, beginning to go numb. I thought that this was it—death. I heard sirens, was braced by the paramedics, and lifted into the back of an ambulance, and when I woke up, I was at Children's Hospital.

They cut off my uniform, and the doctors and nurses said, "You broke your hip and will need surgery to repair it."

They cut open my leg and put metal screws in my hip to hold it together, then stitched me back up. However, the doctors and nurses also noticed Shirley's handiwork—the scars and welts that decorated my body and could not be explained away: the one I still bear on my face from the time Ralph finally stood up for me, the one on my chest where it had been split open by that belt buckle, and several dozen others from other beatings on my backside, frontside, legs, and arms.

They started asking questions, and for the first time, I thought my voice would be heard. After some prodding, I broke open like a breached dam. Everything came pouring out through tears—the beatings, the way Shirley kept the food locked away in that damned deep freezer, how she tormented me for being sexually abused and said that I had invited and deserved it, and what happened after the magic of visiting cousins went away. I told them I was afraid to go back, that I didn't want to go back. I was so scared, surrounded by all these White people who looked concerned, all of them promising that they would take care of me, telling me that my life was valuable. Then, after some back and forth with the court system and case workers, they did what they said they would not do: they sent me back.

When I returned home six weeks later, Shirley and I had a talk.

"You can take your ass to live in an orphanage," she said.

"I didn't tell them anything," I said. But they had too many details, details that Shirley denied but knew were true.

"So, you had to have talked," she said. "You can live in an orphanage where you'll be shuttled from facility to facility. You think living with me is tough; you'll be abused again," she said.

Shirley and everyone around me had put the fear of God in me about the orphanage. They had described it as like being a prison, where the abuse would be worse than anything I could imagine. So, I stayed with Shirley. Shirley's abuse was different this time. It was better. She said things like, "You deserved to be sexually abused," and "You ain't gone be shit," and, of course, "You are a stupid motherfucker."

Later, I asked Shirley for a curl, a popular hairstyle, and she said, "No, you can have a perm."

I got the perm, and she made me think it was close to a curl, particularly if I curled my hair with small rollers. Then, she threatened to "send my bitch ass to school in a dress." I was teased in school because boys didn't perm their hair. Shirley found delight in that taunting. I later learned that this was called emotional abuse.

For a while after my hip surgery, I moved around in a wheelchair, then on crutches, and then I was back on my bicycle. Caseworkers visited us through the years to check in, but I learned not to trust them, so I was always "fine" when asked how I was doing. Being in fear was my normal state of mind.

I don't think anyone from school knew exactly what was happening in our home, but I was told I was special from an early age. Just how special, I didn't know. Sometimes, I was told, "Boy, you have a learning disorder." Other times, I was told, "Boy, you have a behavior disorder." When I got into Stix, a magnet school in the city, I was told, "Stix is a school for gifted kids." I was confused.

From Stix, I went to Mason, a mixed-raced junior high. While at Mason, I found a friend in a gentleman from our church named Mr. Tillman. When I got in trouble at school for getting into a fight, there was no way in hell I would call Shirley. I knew she'd find out eventually, but I preferred that it be later rather than sooner. So, I called Mr. Tillman, and he came to school and spoke to the principal. Mr. Tillman understood me. He knew things weren't the best at home, but despite his intercession, he couldn't stop me from being suspended.

For the next three days, I spent all my school time hanging out at Barrett Brothers Park in North Saint Louis. I would get up, make like I was going to school, and retrieve my bicycle I'd hidden the night before in the brush adjacent to the house. I would take the alley, coast downhill toward Saint Louis Avenue, and duck down when passing my house, heart racing. I'd pedal like I was in a race for my life up the hill on Saint Louis Avenue toward Goodfellow, less than one mile from my home. When I got to the park, my heartbeat would normalize because I felt safe; I knew Shirley would never come to the park. She was overweight and had other health problems that kept her close to home. Besides, she needed to be at the house to feed Ora, take her to dialysis, and empty her shit pot when I wasn't around to do it.

During the summers and on some school days, I would wake early to ride with Ora on Call-A-Ride to her dialysis and then catch the bus to school nearby. There was freedom and safety on the bus—the same freedom and safety I felt when I rode my bike to the park. Like the bus, the park felt *contained*, a green, irregular space at the corner of Goodfellow Boulevard and Saint Louis Avenue. It had been named for White, Irish immigrant brothers who had once lived nearby, a reminder that my "ghetto" neighborhood used to be a mostly White, working-class part of the city. All day, I slept lying flat on the ground in the shade, walked around, and sometimes played basketball with other kids who'd ditched school or weren't in school anymore. And I rode my bicycle. It was three days of being like a regular kid.

I COULD HAVE KILLED HIM. When I was thirteen years old and still living with Shirley, I got into a fight in the alley up the street from my home. I was a troubled kid in many ways, and up to that point, I'd gotten into plenty of fights. However, what made this altercation stand out was it was the first time I can remember wanting to kill someone other than myself. I can't remember why we were fighting, but I'm certain that it was nonsense, agitated by the fact that there was a crowd watching.

I don't know what came over me to think about ending that kid's life, but I'm glad I made a different decision.

The other kid was about my age but a little bigger, stronger, and faster. We both landed some blows and ended in a tussle. He was pinned down to the ground, and I straddled him. I was having one of those out-of-body experiences where I could feel the blood pumping through my veins. My thoughts were clouded.

My adrenaline was in overdrive. All I could think about was what this kid would do to me if I let him up. So, in one second, I suspended my judgment, grabbed a brick, and held it over his head.

In that same second, I asked myself, *What are we fighting for?* I don't know what came over me to think about ending that kid's life, but I'm glad I made a different decision. At that moment, I realized what I was capable of doing. Later, after reflecting on the situation, I determined that murder was incompatible with the life I wanted.

However, it didn't take much to set me off, and I struggled with being unable to control my temper, impulses, and life. I was hypersensitive. I believed that any external threat was intended for my destruction—even if it took the form of small violations. Once, I hit a kid in the face so hard for stealing a fifty-cent bag of chili cheese Fritos that I'd bought for a girl I liked. I worked hard for that money, but I didn't feel good after I hit him—not to mention I shattered my writing hand, and it ballooned as much as his forehead in a matter of seconds. His face was unrecognizable—just like mine when Shirley hit me in the face with the belt buckle. Though I didn't like hitting this kid, I felt like he didn't respect me. He took my chips, which were my currency with this girl, and that was a slippery slope.

THE FIRST AND ONLY VIDEO GAME CONSOLE I ever owned was an Atari that I purchased around 1985. I had saved my money—more than one hundred dollars—by working odd jobs. I set a goal to purchase it, and I did. At the start of my eighth-grade year, I bought an Adidas suit—black with white stripes—with my money. It was 1989, and this was the coolest outfit I'd ever owned. That Adidas suit helped me gain some sense of coolness and acceptance among my peers. I was a depressed, unsure, introverted kid who felt more comfortable around old people. Older people were less judgmental about my life and my predicament as an intense, poor foster kid without a sense of style. I never had cool clothes or shoes.

I worked and did whatever I could to earn money. When I worked, it meant I could eat when I wanted. Instead of sleeping in, I shoveled snow when we had snow days. I got up, bundled up in sweatpants and jeans, used socks as gloves, and knocked on doors.

When asked, "Baby, how much do you charge?"

I always said, "Maim [it was mostly women who answered the doors], whatever you can spare is fine."

Some would take advantage of me and only give me five dollars to shovel what looked like a football-length staircase and sidewalk. Others would be more generous. It always worked out. By noon, I had a pocket full of money. I was a saver, so I loved how my pocket bulged and how I felt after two back-to-back snow days, which were rare. I liked having money.

I also cut grass during the summer. I made a deal with Mr. Wallace down the street. Mr. Wallace lived by himself, but his mother and sister lived within two doors.

"Mr. Wallace," I said, "I will cut your grass for free if you allow me to use your lawnmower to cut Mrs. Jackson's house and some others."

He agreed, and we shook on it. The only house I saw built from the ground up was just up the street. I thought whoever lived in that house must be rich; they were on a double lot. I knocked on that door to cut their grass, too.

I also spent long, hot days turning soil and pulling weeds in preparation for planting new seeds. Mr. Wallace's mother had a garden in her backyard, and he paid me to work in it sometimes. It was backbreaking work.

One summer, Shirley introduced me to Mr. Weeden. Mr. Weeden owned a construction company and a daycare in Wellston on a street called Dr. Martin Luther King Drive. At one point, Wellston had a streetcar and was a shopping district. Mr. Weeden let me shadow him as a favor to Shirley. We took long trips on the highway to pick up supplies. Mr. Weeden sometimes fell asleep, and then he'd wake up all excited.

"Mr. Weeden, are you OK?" I softly asked when I thought he'd fallen asleep.

I didn't want to startle him, but I had to do something to wake him up because the speedometer was nearing 70 mph. With Mr. Weeden, I carried wood to other workers and cleaned up junk. Once, we had to tear down a penny candy store. To my surprise, it was dark, musty, and wet when we went in, but there was still some candy there.

"Take all you want," Mr. Weeden said.

And I did. I filled my pockets and belly.

I worked hard whenever I could. Sometimes, I didn't get paid with money, but one of my customers said, "Stop by anytime you need a sandwich." Someone else, an elderly woman, took me to Veterans Village, a local thrift shop, to get some clothes. And they were better than the clothes we found in the alley! I also got clothes and food from the church.

Other forms of goodwill paid off, too. Once, I was chased by a group of gang members, and I stepped into a ditch and hobbled while I was running. I could see Mr. Wallace, who stood perched over the front of his porch most days to see what was happening from both directions, coming down the street as quickly as he could with his pistol in tow. I ran past my house to his porch while he shouted, "You motherfuckers leave this kid alone!" while pumping his pistol in the air. When the coast was clear, I hobbled home, went to the emergency room, and learned that I had broken my foot.

Saint Edwards King Catholic Church on the corner of Clara and Maffit was where we worshipped and participated in vacation Bible school. I served as an altar boy assisting the priest during Mass and sometimes worked. I worked one summer with Mr. Tillman in a program designed to keep us kids off the streets. It was when the Bloods and Crips were on the rise. By this time, gang violence, crack cocaine, and teenage pregnancy were all the talk. The church wanted us to avoid all that stuff. One of the neighborhood kids I knew from school (he'd been a part of the group that chased me) couldn't have been thirteen years old, but he drove by us in his car while we were cleaning the church lot. He strutted out in his dope man shoes, the classic Nike Cortez shoes popularized by its association with gang culture and frequent appearance in hip-hop songs. For instance, NWA (Niggas with Attitudes) had a hit song with the same name released in 1987. He glanced over at us and chuckled, but he was eventually sent to prison. A typical conversation among us kids was about who was murdered or who was in jail. On the corner of Saint Louis Avenue and Arlington, someone had recently "gotten their head blew off." We saw the blood-stained concrete that never seemed to fade. I had to watch my back because I wasn't a part of a gang.

I didn't have time to join a gang. On Saturdays, I volunteered at the church. We met early to go to the Schnucks market warehouse, our hometown grocer, where I had my first W-2 job, to collect expired pastries, bread, and other food items. I cherished these Saturdays, packing boxes for some elderly neighbors on my block and keeping one for myself. Carrying as much as I could down the alley for half a mile, I visited Mrs. Jackson's house first, then Mr. Wallace's, and distributed treats before I returned home to heat up the pastries and eat until I was full. We browsed through donated clothes on Sundays after Mass and chose what we wanted.

I was bussed to the Academy of Math and Science during my freshman year in high school. In high school, the cool kids and upperclassmen claimed seats at the back of the bus (the irony of this in light of civil rights!). In an act of defiance that seemed to be a marker in my life, I decided to sit at the back of the bus because there was no one up front with whom I wanted to sit. A tall, scrawny upperclassman with nice clothes and shoes got on the bus, and he shot a disapproving and aggressive look in my direction.

"Yo punk ass needs to move out of my seat," he said, pointing at my Veteran's village clothes and shoes and laughing.

I ignored him and acted confidently as though he wasn't talking to me. This was the first week in school; he couldn't be talking to me.

"If you sit back here tomorrow, I am going to beat yo ass," he said.

He had mistaken me for someone else as he dapped his friends, who continued laughing and egging him on. My friend from the neighborhood was on the bus and was sitting up front. Cornelius was his name, the same as my little brother. I wondered if it came down to blows if he would help. *I would if the role was reversed*, I thought as I stared out the window.

The next day, I didn't have a choice but to sit in the back. Otherwise, I'd have problems with bullies from that point on. *May as well put an end to this shit*, I thought. To my surprise, nothing happened. However, a few days later, when I felt comfortable and relaxed, we pulled to the front of the school, and I grabbed my backpack and stood up. Then, I felt it. His fists started raining down on me, one after the other, and I retreated into a sitting and ducking position.

I heard the bus driver say, "Stop it!" and then he radioed for support.

I immediately regained my composure, lunged, and wrapped my arms around the other kid to stop the blows. Then, I commenced to beat his ass. One blow after another, I would not stop even though I was tired. It was well beyond whipping him and defending myself—I wanted to send a message. I was raging and out of control and went crazy on this kid until the bus driver pulled me off him. I was bloody, but so was he. I hadn't seen it coming, but he saw all of me coming.

The school security guard escorted me to the nurse's office and then off to see the principal. I received an in-school suspension, and the school counselor, Mrs. Kennedy, connected me with an older, offsite mentor and some other boys who were upperclassmen. As the rumor mill swirled, I got the daps from everybody for defending myself. My neighborhood friend didn't help me, but that was OK because that other kid never looked my way again. I didn't have many problems after that because everyone knew I could hold my own, and they were smart enough to leave me alone. *Message delivered,* I thought. That was the second-to-last time I felt the need to fight with my hands. What I needed to learn was how to fight with my mind.

SEVERAL YEARS LATER, AFTER hip surgery, many fights, broken bones, and emotional abuse, I got off the school bus at the corner of Saint Louis Avenue and Semple. I heard what I thought was our house alarm going off in the background. I looked up the street and saw the rotating lights of an ambulance. I frantically ran up the block. I couldn't imagine what could be wrong; Shirley always had things under such tight control. I jumped the ledge into the yard, ran up to the front porch and through the door, and was met by a stunning sight.

Shirley, this powerful, towering woman, was lying on the floor—immobile, unresponsive, and not so powerful.

"Do you have the code to the house alarm?" the paramedic asked.

Of course, I didn't. Shirley would never trust us with the code to the house alarm, and if she saw me messing with it, she would come to a full stand and slap the hell out of me. So, no, I didn't know the code, but I had seen her enter it so many times that I'd memorized the pattern. I started stabbing methodically at the box. Finally, somehow, I hit it. The alarm stopped.

I realized then that the smoke filling the house had set off the alarm. Apparently, Shirley had passed out while frying something. She ate a lot of fried food. Luckily, the alarm brought the first responders to the house quickly enough to turn off the stove before the house caught on fire. As they placed her on the stretcher and rolled her out the door, her eyes were open, but she was still speechless.

Two or three weeks earlier, the three of us kids had been home alone because, by this time, Ora had died. When we heard Shirley's car arrive, we straightened up in a hurry and frantically got back into the places where Shirley told us to stay put. We listened for the usual: first, the car door would open, and it did; second, the screen door would creak open, but this didn't happen, and there was no sound of her key in the lock. We waited, frozen by fear in our places, and wondered if Shirley was trying to catch us doing something—catch us doing anything—so she could cuss us out. After what seemed like hours, I risked looking out the window. I saw Shirley's car and what I thought was a leg on the ground, but the retaining wall in the front obstructed my view. It was cold and icy outside, so we wondered if Shirley had taken a fall. We were afraid to open the door because Shirley would "beat our Black asses" if we opened that door for any reason. So, we waited. We couldn't use the phone; she had most things rigged so she could tell if we messed with it. After a while, my younger brother and I unlocked the front door to get a closer look. Shirley was lying on the ground, and we helped her to her feet and into the house. We never spoke of it; we assumed she slipped and hit her head.

"So, what's wrong with her?" I asked the paramedic.

"I'm not sure—probably an aneurysm," he answered.

"What's an aneurysm?" I asked.

"It's when a blood vessel pops in your brain," he said.

Still confused, I knew Shirley's situation was serious. I asked if I could go to the hospital. I hopped inside the ambulance and rode to the hospital with them. There, Shirley was admitted and taken to surgery. It was strange to see her lying alone at the mercy of tubes and machines and strangers.

For several months after that, my siblings and I lived in the house by ourselves.

"It was a stroke," they confirmed. The stroke didn't kill her, but she would never come home again.

"Shirley is incapacitated," the social worker later said.

I wondered if her earlier fall had something to do with Shirley's condition or if the fall was an early warning sign. I didn't know, but it occupied my thoughts.

For several months after that, my siblings and I lived in the house by ourselves. Church members brought food by. We had fried chicken, baked ham, and turkey and ate all we wanted. One day, social workers showed up and said we could no longer live alone. We needed to be cared for.

We learned that Shirley's sister had called the Division of Family Services. They surveyed our relationships and found homes for each of us. None of us moved in with members of Shirley's family, reinforcing Shirley's point to Ralph: "If you care so much, then you take him," to which Ralph and no one else ever stepped in to save us. No one cared that much; we were too much charity.

I moved up the street to my best friend's grandmother's house—Ms. Jackson's. She was a good woman. She had a daughter two years younger than me and a grandson, who was probably a year younger but in one grade higher, who lived with her. He was my best friend through the years. During summers, we'd wake early and be outside playing football, court (a game similar to stickball), and basketball. The milk-crate hoop was affixed to a tree in the alley. We played there, trying not to twist our ankles on the uneven pavement while using the base of the tree as an explosive launch pad to dunk the ball. If you hit the tree just right to catapult yourself into the air, you felt like an NBA player, screaming "and one" with the slightest tap. On occasions when I was allowed to stay over, we'd be up all-night playing video games and eating late-night egg sandwiches smothered in butter or huge bowls of cereal.

Moving up to Ms. Jackson's, I thought, would bring more of those good times, but I lived with them for less than six months. When the state was deciding about my permanent placement, they asked me if I wanted to live with Ms. Jackson. I said no. She was willing to have me, but I was not willing to stay.

Her daughter had once said to me in the heat of some argument, "At least I have a mom."

She knew about my mother's death. She knew I didn't have anyone who cared about me, and those words devastated me. So, when asked if I wanted to stay with them, I said no. I preferred to be around people who couldn't say such things to me. I know we were kids, and she didn't know what she was saying, but I'd already lived a life of trauma.

This time, I would choose the trauma that I subjected myself to. I chose an orphanage—Annie Malone Children's Home. It was lonely, but this was my choice. This decision taught me that I would do what I needed to do to take care of my emotional health.

KIDS CRY OUT

Each day we take a moment
And reflect on our purpose
We're dedicated to the mission
We're dedicated to the service
The universal bond
That all people share
Is that they once cried out
And needed someone else to care

Children
This world's most valuable asset
Are being abused and neglected
By adults
Whose job it is to
Love and protect

The decay in a child's life
Prompts us to stay strong
God is sure to answer our prayers
If we continue to press on

Kids cry out in a world
In which
They are unable to fend for themselves
Enduring exploitation
And misfortune
As they journey the trail

The scars that they carry
Rips at the seam
The very essence of their soul
That binds them to their dreams

Kids cry out
Every second
Of every minute
Of every hour
Of every year
And as long as this is the case
Our mission in life should be clear

CHAPTER 4

"I don't know what God has planned for me or you or anyone,
but I do know that in darkness, you discover an indistinguishable light."

— Cory Booker

After Shirley's illness, I tried to figure out how to channel my aggression. I was still an explosive kid when the circumstances warranted, and my explosive reactions exposed a core weakness that left me unprotected from the condemnation and consequences that often came along with those eruptions. I would get so angry when pushed that I would shake like my first car did—an '87 Buick LeSabre—when I opened her up on the highway. I had to hold tightly to the wheel to keep control of it.

I often asked myself if, in the long run, my explosiveness had benefitted me in any way. And I realized that I couldn't be my own enemy. I ultimately didn't like who I became when that part of me was triggered, and I knew I needed to take control. Most people don't want to be around others who are easily set off and volatile, and I needed to control myself.

I learned that aggression and passion have similar features but different outcomes. While aggression is often uncontrolled and off-putting, passion taps into the same emotion more productively. I learned to harness aggression and anger and channel them into productive passion, which ultimately helped me become a better person. Passion inspires hope; aggression inspires fear. This was evident as I started writing my thoughts in poetry and rhymes.

I developed a habit of speaking slowly and prioritizing others in conversation to channel my aggression into passion. This approach allowed me to communicate clearly and honestly, fostering connections and uplifting those around me. Despite the challenge of having my kindness misinterpreted as a weakness, I found the inner strength to remain composed without reacting impulsively.

I discovered that if I wasn't in a life-or-death situation, I could refrain from speaking, think, and slow things down, and most situations aren't life or death. When I felt attacked, my initial words in a heated moment weren't necessarily words of life but words intended to inflict the same pain that was aimed in my direction. So, I became quick to think and slow to speak.

I developed a habit of speaking slowly and prioritizing others in conversation to channel my aggression into passion.

"The only thing you control in any exchange is your reaction," my therapist said. "You don't always control how it makes you feel or what it makes you think, but you can control your reaction."

That's what helped me decide to leave Ms. Jackson's home. I learned that I should seek to build others up, not tear them down, and sometimes, "you just have to remove yourself" from a situation, as my therapist said. By building others up, I could grow connections. In other words, aggression channeled appropriately could be a powerful tool to inspire.

Discovering my key triggers greatly improved my ability to pre-emptively address conversations that were heating up and effectively manage my surroundings. This awareness allowed me to take moments to reflect, gather different perspectives, and pay attention to a more uplifting inner voice instead of the one compelling me to, "Don't take shit from nobody." By adopting a slower pace in my responses and embracing a generous attitude in my conversations, I found myself listening with the intention to truly understand, thus enhancing the conversation's quality. This approach steered me away from reacting out of raw emotion and toward engaging with a mindful enthusiasm, aiming to influence others to see, think, or act in a different way. It's a hard thing, for sure, when you're a small boy, and you realize that you must fend for yourself if you're going to survive. It's easy to lose hope when you perceive limited options based on your age and stage in life. It's easy to lose hope when, even if you know you're alone, you don't have any personal agency or control over your life.

TODAY, WE WITNESS DISCONNECTED KIDS and adults who lack self-control and easily come unhinged over the slightest offense. We see people who feel like they've lost control of their environment, future, and country; some view themselves as victims. Perceived scarcity of opportunity and economic, racial, and political differences have sent many skidding into one ditch after another. We've devolved into a nation of finger-pointers who assign blame to others for what we believe is our circumstance.

I believe that each of us must take ownership of ourselves and our emotions. That's the first step to taking more control over your environment. You are responsible for yourself. I am responsible for me—and we should all be held accountable for negative behavior that impacts others. It's taken me a while to get here because I had no firm foundation for what was right and wrong. I only knew that you were either the victim or the victimizer, either by choice or by chance.

I struggled with internal criticism. Despite being naturally kind as a child, I worried others might see it as a weakness. Early abuse made me very cautious in my interactions. I often withdrew from relationships to avoid getting hurt. I was self-conscious about my appearance, especially the scar, and chose bus seats where I felt less exposed. These feelings were hard to overcome, partly because I struggled to counter nega-

I believe that each of us must take ownership of ourselves and our emotions. That's the first step to taking more control over your environment.

tive thoughts. My reaction to perceived threats sometimes made me overly defensive, leading to isolation and harshness toward myself and others. To address this, I needed to recognize specific triggers, such as:

- Lack of control or choice from my childhood
- Challenges with timed tests
- Feeling exploited or taken advantage of
- Experiencing or perceiving threats or bullying
- Concerns that my kindness might be seen as weakness
- Frustration with unfair treatment
- Feeling protective when seeing loved ones in distress

Understanding these triggers, which still affect me, has been crucial. Recognizing our triggers is key to addressing them.

Growing up in a violent environment nurtured my propensity for violence. To survive, I matched the intensity around me. I saw others fly off the handle, so I did too. I saw others break into homes, so I broke into a home. These were choices based on my perceived options. My mother's death was the ultimate loss of control. Years later, when my brother was paralyzed, I was reminded that I was always one wrong decision away from the life I was statistically supposed to live. These events constantly reminded me to reflect on my journey.

DESPITE ALL I'D BEEN TOLD ABOUT ORPHANAGES, I decided to go to the Annie Malone Children's Home. I was fifteen years old when my siblings and I permanently went our separate ways. My case worker told me that my younger brother went to the Emergency Children's Home (ECHO) on North Euclid at this time, which would later be my final group home as a foster kid. Though I wasn't certain, I believed my sister went to

Entering residential care, I felt as though I was sinking further into America's underbelly. . . I came to see myself as a child of the sewers.

Marian Hall, an all-girls home, before she bounced around to several other homes, including a crossover stint with me at Annie Malone.

Entering residential care, I felt as though I was sinking further into America's underbelly, a sentiment reinforced by Shirley's treatment, which stripped away any hope for something better. I came to see myself as a child of the sewers. My parents' lack of self-worth had become my own. Inside me, two voices battled: one convinced me I was "less than," undeserving of parents, love, or any semblance of goodness, even if it were offered directly by God. The other voice clung to a thread of hope, yearning for meaning, connection, and a sense of belonging.

Just as quickly as I'd fallen into the foster care system, I fell from kinship care to this group home setting. *Life is so unfair,* I often thought. I was ashamed to let my friends from school know that I'd moved to a group home with other boys and girls and that I had no family. I felt guilty that maybe I'd done something to deserve or cause my circumstances, or maybe Mom had died because of me. I was angry that I didn't have parents to do things with me like normal kids did. Most of all, I was afraid. I feared that I would end up like my parents—poor and unprepared for life's challenges—and that I would never have anyone to love me.

My brokenness as a child was not my own doing. I hadn't made the decisions that produced my traumatic experiences, and it was important for me to embrace this truth so I could move through the darkness and fog that became my days and nights after Shirley was incapacitated. *As children, we are beholden to the adults in our lives,* I repeated to myself over and over again as I prepared for my ride to Annie Malone. The more I said it, the more I thought I'd believe it so I wouldn't feel shame, guilt, or fear of being judged—all emotions I had to grapple with as I mentally prepared myself.

In some ways, I believed I was one of the unluckiest kids. I was born in an East Saint Louis town that had seen better days, and I was raised all over North City in neighborhoods that seemed to extract their pound of flesh—in a broader part of the region that was down on its luck, too. *Here I go again,* I thought. Shirley had beaten a robot-like compliance into me. What scars would this new place leave? *I'm older now,* I thought. *Nothing happens to me that I don't want to happen to me, damn it, and I mean it!* My heart had hardened. I was now traveling to another wrong zip code but to a neighborhood that had a tremendous history, an organization that Black people revered—Annie Malone. After talking to my social worker, I knew I had to show up differently to be successful in this institution. That was fine because I'd been practicing self-restraint for a while now.

I stuffed my plastic bags, said my goodbyes to the Jacksons, and loaded them and myself into the social worker's car. At this point, I'd lost everything. Every important relationship, however dysfunctional, was now gone. As I made the two-and-a-half-mile trip east to the Annie Malone Children's Home, my surroundings didn't change too much, but I knew I was about to enter a new world. Annie Malone is in the heart of The Ville, a neighborhood that is the historical home of Saint Louis's Black middle class. I didn't know what middle class was, but it looked like more people lived in homes—and that was always a signal to me that they had food. Like the neighborhood I came from, The Ville had solid brick homes that lined the streets. Some were single-family buildings, some were two- or four-family flats, and most had been built in the first twenty or thirty years of the twentieth century. However, they were showing their age. Weeds covered some vacant lots, and some buildings looked like they were about to fall in, but as we turned north onto Annie Malone Drive, an impressive brick building loomed ahead. It looked like a mansion to me, covering a little less than a block.

"Wow," I said, "it looks like that house on television." I was referencing the White House. It had four big white pillars that supported a portico over the entrance. I couldn't believe that this was about to become my new home. *The people who own that home must be rich*, I thought. At this point, I knew I'd have to work even harder to make it.

Nearby, evidence of The Ville's history continued. The land owned by Annie Malone and the surrounding streets had once belonged to a White man named Charles Elleard. He built a nursery on his property, and a community gradually grew around it, like the plants that flourished in his greenhouses. It became known as Elleardsville. According to Tim Fox in *Where We Live: A Guide to St. Louis Communitie*s, in 1876, the city of Saint Louis annexed the land, and German, Irish, and Black working-class people started putting down roots. The African American presence continued to grow with the addition of Elleardsville Colored School No. 8 in 1873 and

Saint James African Methodist Episcopal Church in 1885. A quarter-century later, residents had shortened the town's name to The Ville, and Sumner High School had moved to West Cottage Avenue from downtown. Notable figures such as Tina Turner, Robert Guillaume, Arthur Ashe, and Dick Gregory attended the school. Its stately red brick building still stands and serves students across the street from Annie Malone Children's Home. It was the first high school for African American kids west of the Mississippi.

Just east of the Children's home stood the massive Homer G. Phillips Hospital. The two buildings nearly touch even today. The hospital opened in 1937 amid The Ville's transformation into a neighborhood for a growing and solid Black middle class. The neighborhood's population changed from 8 percent Black to 95 percent Black between 1920 and 1950. According to author Tim Fox, Homer G. Phillips was a milestone, "the largest and best health care facility in the world committed to the care of African American patients and the training of African American doctors and nurses." The V-shaped building designed by Albert Osberg is now a nursing home, but it looks as solid and immovable as the day it was built.

Another early twentieth-century institution in The Ville was Poro College, also a stone's throw from my new home. Poro College was the first headquarters of Poro Beauty Products at 4300 Saint Ferdinand Avenue. The company catered to the nation's—and The Ville's—growing African American community, which could afford hair-straightening and other beauty products. In *That's the Way It Was,* a collection of oral histories by middle-class Black Saint Louisans, Salimah Jones describes the problem she faced as a teenager growing up in the City's Mill Creek Valley neighborhood in the 1950s:

> I remember once in high school a White girl asked, "Why do you straighten your hair?" We explained it was because

our hair is originally in tight curls, and we made a joke that first you get a pressing comb and you heat it up on this big fire, and when you take it off, there's all of this blue smoke. And that's how it really does look to the child, all this blue smoke is around the comb. You wipe it with a cloth or something, to kind of cool it down, and then you oil the hair, and you take this hot comb . . . and straighten the hair, and the hair would come out *very* straight. . . . You know, combing hair like mine is hard. As a kid, you call kids 'tender headed' who didn't like to have their hair combed, because the comb pulls through their hair and it hurts. . . . Sometimes people say you want to be White; I don't think it's wanting to be White, I think it's wanting what's easy, and good hair was easy hair. It required less care.

Yes, life was easier with "good hair," and the Poro company's hair straightening product could make life a little bit easier for an African American woman with "bad hair." However, the only way to get the product was to have a little extra money to spend. Again, the Poro company's success went against the common notion of a single Black community. Clearly, a significant number of African American people of some means had to be living not only in Saint Louis but also across the country for companies like Poro to succeed. The visionary behind Poro College and its successful line of hair care products, Annie Minerva Turnbo Pope Malone, recognized this, and it made her one of the most unlikely millionaires in history. She was also the namesake of my new home in The Ville.

According to the State Historical Society of Missouri website, Annie Turnbo Malone was born in Metropolis, Illinois. Orphaned as a child, she was raised by her older sister among nine siblings. With a talent for chemistry and keen observation of her African American community's needs, Malone invented her signature hair-straightening product. In 1902, she relocated to Saint Louis and expanded her business by recruiting sales-people to promote products door-to-door. At the 1904 World's Fair, she sold her products, marking the start of her national expansion. In 1914, she married Aaron Malone and became a Black female millionaire within four years, establishing Poro College with a training facility and company headquarters. The college employed around two hundred locals at its peak and became a hub of community pride with amenities such as a post office and an auditorium that featured performances by artists like Ethel Waters. It also hosted the National Negro Business League's headquarters. In 1927, when a tornado struck, the American Red Cross used the college as a relief center. Poro College went beyond cosmetology and offered courses in literature, drama, and music to provide a compre-hensive curriculum.

By the 1950s, the training model Malone pioneered at Poro College had expanded to thirty-two branches nationwide. Her business and fortune continued to prosper. Although she had relocated the business to Chicago in 1930, she never for-got Saint Louis or the feeling of being orphaned at a young age. One of the many charities she supported was the Saint Louis Colored Orphans Home. According to the Associated Charitable Workers' Register of Charities in Saint Louis in 1889, the Saint Louis Colored Orphans Asylum was founded in 1888 on 12th Street in downtown Saint Louis. It catered to the numerous homeless African American children who were wandering the streets without care. White children had access to more resources like the House of Refuge, the Woman's Humane Society of Missouri (dedicated to protecting animals and children from cruelty), the Baptist Orphans' Home, the Methodist Orphans' Home, the German Evangelical Lutheran Orphan Asylum, or the German Protestant Orphans' Home. In 1901, the Saint Louis Colored Orphans Home moved to a house on Natural Bridge, but by 1919, it had been condemned.

That year, Annie Malone became president of the home's board of directors. As head of the organization, she not only moved the home to The Ville and saved it from bankruptcy but also leveraged its proximity to Poro College to make it a year-round cultural heart for the community. Its Christmas parties for the orphans were legendary. In the late 1930s, a Stowe Teachers College sorority, the Girl Scouts, the Brownies, the University City Chauffeur's Club, and the DeMun Avenue Community School all joined in to present the kids with gifts and holiday celebrations. In the spring, the home's May Day Parade, started in 1910, would draw thousands of participants and spectators; in 1940, there were 3,000 participants and 12,000 people cheering them on, according to the *St. Louis Argus* newspaper. Three years after her tenure as board president ended, she gave $10,000 of Poro profits to buy the land for a new Black orphanage building at 2612 Goode Avenue. At that time, Annie Malone's business empire was at its peak. When the new Saint Louis Colored Orphans Home was dedicated as the Annie Malone Children's Home in 1946, it continued the original home's traditions of community participation and support. The Annie Malone May Day Parade is still held in downtown Saint Louis.

As we pulled up in front of the Annie Malone Home, I said to myself, *One day, I'll own a home like this, maybe in a community like this.*

A LOT OF THINGS WERE FAMILIAR to me. One street in front of us, Kennerly, triggered me because I'd once lived on that street with Mom, and Tandy Rec Center was where I learned how to box when I was younger. I walked between those big white columns and through the front door of the Annie Malone Children's Home with all my belongings and trash bags full of clothes. At the initial checkpoint, the social worker exchanged some information with the attendant.

"Orvin Kimbrough, permanent placement," she mumbled. We then made our way down a hallway to check in with the woman who would become one of my counselors, Mrs. Heron. I was short on words.

"How are you, Orvin?" she asked.

"I'm fine," I said, not willing to say anything more.

I wasn't fine. I was afraid, and I was angry at Shirley's family. *I don't have anyone*, I thought as I marveled at the size of the facility, now my new home.

After check-in, I was escorted up the big staircase. On the second-floor landing, I could see that the building was split in two—the north and south halves were mirror images of each other. I would live in the North Dorm, while the younger kids, later including my little sister, lived in the South Dorm. The living areas were along the stairs on either side, with a small bathroom off each, where the children showered together from a single spigot. The dorm rooms were further divided into east and west rooms, each with up to six beds. The floor had black and white tile arranged like a chess board, and small closets held whatever belongings we came with. Each room had a bell in it, which I soon learned would sound when it was time to change activities—go to class, go to art class, eat—and an intercom system delivered announcements.

I continued up to the third floor. The first room to the left belonged to me and my roommate. A window overlooked the playground, and that was where we would sit and watch the younger kids running around outside and wait for our turn to go out. Groups rarely co-mingled. The closet was bigger than the second floor's, and we had separate shower stalls. But the bells were still there, symbolizing the loving control Annie Malone would have over my life.

For the first time, I encountered a point system that correlated levels and privileges with behavior. Level three represented the highest honor, granting the chance to go on home visits if you had a "resource," the clinical term for someone in the community willing to take you for a weekend, engage in outdoor activities, work, or watch TV.

"The goal of the point system, Orvin," my therapist said, "is to help kids learn acceptable behaviors and to have a direct feedback loop to rewards and consequences."

I hated that damn system. It did two things well: when kids were compliant and obedient, all was good, but when children had small infractions, these were sometimes escalated and compounded because all we could see was what they were taking away from us. It was easy to fall into despair and not care about the points at all. *If they were going to take points away from us, then let's really earn the demotion and give 'em hell*, we thought.

While I was basically a good kid and tried to stay at the higher level, I was still a teenager. Within days of arriving, I got into a fight with a boy named Jimmy, a hothead who would later reveal a tender, compassionate side. This was my first fight at Annie Malone and the last fistfight of my youth. As boys, we were testy, and a lot of that was simply a function of our developmental, hormonal stage. A lot of the other kids I remember were girls. There were the Robinson sisters, Miesha and Iesha; Clarisa, who went to Turner Middle School; the short, fair-skinned April (who caught the bus with me) was bound for independent living; and many others who stayed a short while or longer.

I HAD NOTICED GIRLS, like the brown-skinned CC, who liked my friend Ronell when I lived with Shirley on Semple. He and I once got into a fight. I thought it would be just him and me fighting, but that was not the case. All the other Jackson kids jumped in; they were tight in that way. CC was the source of that fight, and I never fought over a girl again.

CC's light-skinned, heavier cousin, Pat, liked me, and she would knock on Shirley's door to see if I could come out to play.

I was always reluctant. I tried not to go out and play because her body reminded me of a shorter, light-skinned Shirley, and she was fast. Boy, was she more sexually advanced—*downright promiscuous*, I thought. I learned a lot about the intense feelings that led to sex. However, I didn't want to have sex for fear that she would get pregnant. There were a lot of "Babies Having Babies," as the popular R&B song by Terry Tate proclaimed. That said, I would go back to my basement room in Shirley's house and rub myself blind. I did exactly as Pat told me, and she was right. If I was patient, I'd get a rush and think to myself, *Boy, that felt great!* It was better than the dry hump in the "Catch a Girl, Get a Girl" game I played earlier as a younger kid. I had to hand wash the sock along with my other clothes.

I was somewhat of a late bloomer when it came to acting on my desires with girls, at least compared to the kids I hung out with. To hear them tell it, everybody was "getting some," except me. I was too afraid of the disease that seemed rampant—pregnancy. This struck fear in me.

The first girl I wrote a love letter to was Angel. Angel lived down the block from where we lived with Mom on Wabada. She had the sweetest face; I was in love with this girl. I would walk up Wabada in hopes of getting a glimpse of her. At Annie Malone, however, girls were ever present. When they walked into the room, you couldn't help but look and have your hormones shooting fireworks, but you had to be careful because the source of your erection—I mean affection—could be someone's sister. You never knew.

It was constant teenage teasing. Once, I let on that I liked the girl who rode the bus with me, April. When she walked into the kitchen area with other girls, Jimmy—who could be a hyper, fun-loving kid—jumped up, put his arm on my shoulder, pointed in her direction, and in his loving and intense way said, "There she is, go say something."

"No, Jimmy," I said, scooting down in the seat.

91

"You're a punk," he said.

I looked in April's direction and tried to ignore Jimmy's taunts.

He could barely get the words out because he was laughing so hard, but he shouted, "Orvin likes you, April!"

I didn't think I would rebound from that. But I did rebound, and I did like her. Like me, like Jimmy, she had an optimistic sadness—I couldn't explain it better than that. She was even better company at the bus stop now that she knew I liked her.

Jimmy was always saying something to make me uncomfortable. Once, I was in the shower, chasing that feeling (you know, the feeling, the one that was typically in a sock) when I heard someone walk in, pause by my stall, and burst into laughter. I didn't know who it was until I emerged from the shower and entered the TV room, only to see Jimmy perched on the couch, staring as if he'd caught me doing something unthinkable.

"I saw you," he said in front of the other boys.

"Saw me?" I said. "Saw me doing what?"

He said matter of factly, "You know what," pointing and laughing. "Jacking off," he said.

Not addressing his claim, I said, "If you were watching me in the shower, we should all be laughing at your nasty ass."

Everyone laughed at him. He got mad, but I didn't care. I kept it moving. He was now the butt of the joke that he started. I was certain I wasn't the only kid on the planet who figured out I could reward myself for good behavior—not messing with the girls.

Together, all these kids and I formed a community of kids who understood the pain and uncertainty of life in the foster care system. I had a good group of people watching out for me at Annie Malone. There was Mr. Robinson, my young, African American house parent. He went on to become a director at the YMCA, and I'm still in touch with him today. Annie Malone had a basketball court out back, and I spent a lot of time there, watching the best, most explosive players prove their superiority and score points on and off the court. Our basketball hero was Mr. Trice, who had a deadly three-point shot, and Mr. Robinson, who could hold his own. They also talked serious trash as they played against us kids. Together, these people became a sort of family to me. They provided the consistency and predictability that I craved, and they tried to make Annie Malone as homelike as possible.

Together, all these kids and I formed a community of kids who understood the pain and uncertainty of life in the foster-care system.

The tradition of holiday celebrations that had begun decades before continued while I was there. Sometimes, adults from the community brought us gifts. At Christmas and Thanksgiving, the home filled with the smell of turkey, gravy, and all the fixins'. At times, we would go on outings to places like the YMCA, the Boys & Girls Club, and the Muny—the outdoor municipal theater in Forest Park. I went to my first Saint Louis Cardinals game while at Annie Malone. We sat all the way at the top of Busch Stadium and were allowed to order one hotdog and one soda. We always traveled as a group in the white van with the name "Annie Malone" proudly displayed, and of course, I was self-conscious about people looking at us wherever we went. But it didn't matter. We were happy to be out, seeing the city, stopping at Schnucks for a late-night snack run, and enjoying as normal a life as we could.

However, being "like a family" is not "being a family," and institutional structure is not family structure. In a true family, the members are always around, not just around when their shifts start. At Annie Malone, there were two or three shifts. You had the night workers who worked eight hours. Their main job was to ensure we woke up on time.

"Get up," we heard each morning, "lights on."

We would get up, shower, and go down to the kitchen to eat. There was plenty of food. Then, we went out the door to catch our buses.

Then, there were the day workers. They were around for those of us who either didn't go to school or got into trouble at school. The day workers also took us kids to various external therapy appointments, medical appointments, and court visits.

Finally, the after-school workers ensured we were fed, did homework, got our meds, and were in bed by a certain time.

"Lights out," we often heard yelled from the television room.

In normal families, like that of my best friend Ronell, he could go to family members for anything, at any time—and his grandmother, Ms. Jackson, was the ultimate authority. At Annie Malone, it wasn't that simple. In most cases, we had scheduled time, and then there were policies and procedures, as well as state workers and agency staff, who all were part of the team that made decisions that impacted me. It seemed like there was no ultimate authority.

While in the orphanage, I began to idealize two-parent families. I loved it when I would see a White "resource." I didn't know why, but they were mostly White. Both husband and wife would pick up my roommate, keep him for the weekend, and then drop him back off. He would tell me stories of what he'd done.

"I got to swim. We watched movies. We went to the park. We went to Six Flags," he said.

This is what two-parent families do, I thought. They have fun. I still harbored thoughts that maybe I would get adopted. I felt like I was simply growing older during the days, weeks, and months that I stayed at Annie Malone, not necessarily being cultivated or nurtured. I was always curious about the different personalities and professions of these resources.

"She stays at home, and he does something in business," my roommate would say.

Still, my Annie Malone family did its best, and they cared for us. But did they love us? Maybe, but not how a parent loves a child. Parents punish children to help them grow, while in institutions, counselors punish children for rule-breaking. Parents' discipline is personal and tailored to their child's needs and values, whereas institutional punishment is standardized and applies broadly within the system. Parents, driven by emotional bonds, have a flexible approach, while caregivers in institutional settings are less influenced by such bonds. Parents are flexible; institutions are consistent.

At Annie Malone, rule-breakers and rule-followers were mixed together. I believed some kids misbehaved and broke the law, while kids like me simply lacked parents. I felt like a victim of circumstance, unlike many peers who were victims of their own choices. This resentment and anger grew as I thought about kids with advantages who still ended up there. Why abandon your own family? Today, my perspective has changed.

Despite the structure Annie Malone provided, there was a lot of fear, too. The people I mentioned were wonderful, but there were a lot of adults going in and out that I didn't know; there were too many "anybodies" around. For a kid raised in constant fear of adults, known and unknown, that was traumatic. Annie Malone successfully met my basic needs like food, water, safety, and shelter, but less so in meeting my emotional needs. Sometimes, in addition to my individual therapy, I participated in group therapy, where we worked out our feelings toward each other and tried to understand our identity as growing boys. These were always awkward and superficial because we were unsure of ourselves and lacked confidence. Therefore, if we talked, these were never serious conversations.

My seriousness increased during my time at Annie Malone. I realized I was holding a losing hand. I knew if I didn't establish connections and positive relationships, I wouldn't have much of a life—and I didn't have a plan B. So, for the most part, I set out to work on earning points to move up the level system and did what was expected of me. This had gotten easier for me because I'd worked on taming my temper and cultivating an attitude that was more conducive to drawing people nearer, not pushing them away.

Doing what was expected of me endeared me to some adults. Just like the prior years when I worked odd jobs, I was rewarded if I worked hard for adults. I tried not to create problems, even though my circumstances were problematic. I established positive relationships with house parents and counselors. These were the most powerful and successful people in my life; these were the authority figures. By not creating problems and establishing positive relationships, I received privileges—like being able to exercise and freedom to go outside, on trips, to social activities, and to work.

> *I lived in survival mode, in a hard world where death was a constant companion—and not natural deaths, but early deaths from bad health, lack of access to healthcare, violence, and drugs.*

I created advocates by doing what I was supposed to do. As a kid, I didn't feel that I could make the mistakes most kids made, and if I did, I couldn't afford to be caught. The first time I saw prostitutes and crack cocaine up close—aside from some of my mom's friends and her drugs from a distance—was in the orphanage. By this time, I knew I'd been born in the wrong ZIP Code, and I could understand how whole communities could develop hardened hearts—like mine. I lived in survival mode, in a hard world where death was a constant companion—not natural deaths, but early deaths from bad health, lack of access to healthcare, violence, and drugs. Group homes didn't provide immunity to this. I was also on an emotional roller-coaster, trying not to reveal to the authority figures how much hate I had in me.

I hated my mom, at times, for the childhood that I experienced. I blamed her for dying the way she did, for not protecting me when I was at my most vulnerable, for the many misfortunes in my life, and I blamed my dad for not being there, too. My heart was filled with hatred and self-pity. At one point, I even concluded that it was OK for me to fail because I felt that they let me down, that they had failed me. And my heart grew harder.

The problem is that a hardened heart creates a bitterness that taints how people experience you. It corrupts your perspective, corrodes your being, and is counterproductive to achievement. We cannot give up on life because someone else failed to live it responsibly. The bottom line is that we cannot have a hardened heart if we want to live into God's plan for us. And God has a plan for everyone, I learned, on occasion, when we walked to Antioch Baptist Church just up the road from the orphanage.

By this time, my connection with my siblings was fairly distant. My sister came to Annie Malone—and just like that, she was gone. I had friends in my old neighborhood, Wells Goodfellow, where many kids lived with their mom, grandma, and, on rare occasions, both mother and father. However, I didn't see them much once I went into Annie Malone. Years later, I learned that my best friend Ronell went to prison for something related to drugs. His cousin Red, who lived in North County with his mom in an amazing apartment with a pool, also faced a similar fate. Once, they dared me to jump into the pool's deep end, tap the bottom, and come back up. Despite not knowing how to swim, I took the dare. As I sank, Ronell pulled me out of the water. That night, we ate well as usual, played video games, and never spoke of the incident. We had been best friends when we were younger, thick as thieves. Knowing them and their family intimately, I believe that life might have taken a different turn if they had been introduced to different social circles.

Fortunately, I could still attend the Academy of Math and Science on North Newstead. I never liked it when the school bus dropped me off close to the orphanage. I tried unsuccessfully to keep my new address a secret and asked the bus driver, "Please drop me at the other corner," when I got on the bus.

Ms. Kennedy, the school counselor, continued to be a rock for me during my transition. With her help, I started to find a place in the world. As a freshman and sophomore, I played basketball and wrestled. These were good outlets for me. Once, I got points knocked off because I skipped group therapy so I could go to basketball practice.

I told my therapist, "If I don't practice, I don't play."

This was an example of the rigidity of rules in an institution vs. the flexibility of a functioning two-parent household. I barely got any playing time because I was not a good player, but that was beside the point.

During that first summer, I worked for a landscape company. I got up early, packed a sandwich and plenty of water, and made my way to the pickup location to cut grass with Joe. I worked long days, leaving at dawn and returning to Annie Malone when it was virtually dark. I was exhausted in so many ways. The therapists at Annie Malone insisted I turn my money over to them. I got paid in cash and refused to let go of it. This led to consequences, but again, I didn't care because I didn't want them to control me any more than they already were.

The following year, the Academy of Math and Science closed, and I transferred to Gateway Tech, a big school in the renovated O'Fallon Technical School on McCree Avenue.

At Gateway, I continued playing basketball and added cross-country, not by choice but as a condition to playing basketball. Academically, Gateway had a major advantage that shaped my life: it allowed students to declare a major in subject areas like health careers, math, science, and performing arts. I chose physical therapy because it was a helping profession, and I had a chance to work with the great Erwin Claggett and the Saint Louis University basketball team. Hanging out with the team exposed me to a lot of things I wouldn't have experienced otherwise—especially college life.

One of the significant lessons from my sophomore year was getting kicked off the basketball team for sucking on a Blow Pop before a game.

Coach Bunche burst into the locker room, yelling, "Kimbrough, what's in your mouth?"

"A Blow Pop," I replied, looking at him quizzically.

It was evident I had a Blow Pop in my mouth. *Is the coach OK?* I wondered. He instructed me to get dressed and promptly removed me from the team for breaking the no-eating rule two hours before a game.

I felt furious and looked at him as if he'd lost his mind. I wasn't the only one enjoying a Blow Pop, but he made me the example. So, I left the locker room and never returned. *The injustice*, I thought as I fumed. Some of the other boys snickered at how absurd it was to get kicked off the team for that infraction or that I would allow myself to get caught eating the Blow Pop. That was fine; it gave me more time to work.

Mrs. Kennedy took me to my first job interview with Rosa Grigsby, a Black woman at the Schnucks supermarket at Grand and Gravois in South City.

"She was the store manager," I said to Mrs. Kennedy in amazement. "Oh, by the way, I got the job!"

Mrs. Kennedy just looked at me and smiled, almost as if the interview had been rigged, as if she was the invisible hand.

I would continue to have arguments with Annie Malone about their requirement for me to turn over my check, which had money taken out for state, federal, and union dues. *What the hell is all of this?* I thought. To add insult to injury, Annie Malone wanted me to deposit the check into a checking account, and then they'd give me an allowance. I didn't know what a checking account was. I wanted my money visible to me, like in that Tootsie roll bank.

I LEARNED ABOUT THE Independent Living Program within weeks of arriving at Annie Malone. Independent living was transitional housing for teens who were in foster care. The agency had recently renovated a huge building that was once owned by Homer G. Phillips into other services and apartments for older kids. I needed to be at the agency for a certain amount of time, have the right disposition and motivated attitude, and be seventeen or eighteen to be considered for the program. It was a competitive application process.

My case manager from the state secured me a tour of the facility that had alarm systems, cameras, and locks on everything. Aside from the feeling of being caged, I remember thinking, *These are cool apartments.* More than just the apartments, I welcomed the freedom to come and go as I chose and the additional privileges I'd have if I was accepted into the Independent Living Program. My therapist thought it would be good preparation for independent living if I took some life skills courses through the State of Missouri.

"Life skills?" I said, confused.

"Yes," she answered. "You'll learn about checking, savings, budgeting, interviewing, securing an apartment, transportation—all the stuff that will help you live independently."

Finally, I'm going to learn about where they're putting my money, these so-called checking and savings, I thought.

Life skills courses offered by the Division of Family Services were intended to prepare us older kids for life beyond the group home. A cab picked me up from Annie Malone and took me to a huge government building in downtown Saint Louis called the Wainright Building. There, I joined other kids who were in other group homes from around town or in kinship care. We completed exercises and answered discussion questions intended to increase our literacy about how to navigate the world. The life skill courses were good.

"These are things that most people learn by watching their parents," the instructor would often say.

I learned how to function in society and engage with banking, utilities, landlords, etc., but I also learned that when you meet someone, you need to look that person in the eye and give a firm handshake. It was a "sign of confidence" and the "language of business." *Business,* I thought, *hmmm. That's what Annie Malone, the founder of the home, did; that's what some of the people in suits who come to visit Annie Malone do. Business is what the neighborhood I live in was known for in its heyday!*

This was a huge revelation for me: just by looking someone in the eye, shaking hands, projecting my voice, and speaking clearly, I could make people perceive me as being a confident person. I couldn't believe it at first, and I felt awkward when I first tried it. These skills did not come naturally to me after being systematically abused at every turn. However, the more I practiced, the better I got at it, and my self-concept improved immensely.

During this period, I started hearing words and phrases like, "You have some good leadership skills."

I didn't know what that meant, but I got involved with the newly created Foster Care Youth Advisory Board with Mrs. Thomas. She was a director with the Division of Family Services. That year, we visited Jefferson City and advocated for an increase in our clothing stipend. It was the first time I ever visited our state capital. It was mesmerizing. We succeeded in our advocacy; our annual clothing allowance went from $150 to $200—that number hadn't changed in over a decade. This was a proud moment. *I did that,* I thought.

THE TRUTH OF MY SITUATION started to truly settle in. I wasn't going to be adopted; I was considered too old by this point. People were more inclined to adopt babies and small kids.

I could finish high school, but it would be a real challenge because I was preoccupied with what lay ahead without a family. *How am I going to take care of myself?* I wondered. At this point, I was old enough to grasp the gravity of my circumstances. It was like the time I dared to jump into the deep end of the swimming pool and needed help resurfacing; I felt frozen with insecurity.

The statistics for kids in foster care—whether kinship care, group home, or community living—are not good. In fact, many of them reflect my life. An average of 61 percent of children entering the foster care system test positive for developmental delay—just like I did. Twenty-four percent of foster youth struggle with disabilities while in school—just like I did. Across the United States, 52 percent of foster youth attend schools that rank in the lowest 3 percent—just like I did.

According to Foster Care Facts from the "What Should You Know About Child Abuse" on the Promise2kids site, approximately 50 percent of foster kids will receive a high school diploma. Only 10 percent of former foster youth attend college, and out of that 10 percent, merely 3 percent will graduate. Furthermore, around 50 percent of former foster youth will experience homelessness within the first two years after exiting foster care; roughly 60 percent of girls become pregnant within a few years of leaving the foster care system; 50 percent of youths leaving foster care are unemployed; and 33 percent will receive public assistance.

Before my life skills classes, I didn't know the statistics, but I sensed that my options were limited. If I'd known all these statistics growing up, my self-worth would have been even lower than it was. The problem is that the people who did know these statistics sometimes allowed the disturbing numbers to lower their expectations for foster kids. For example, I wasn't sent to a college preparatory course. I was sent to learn life skills so I could live on my own when I turned eighteen. A lot of people didn't expect me to do anything different than what my parents had done, just as I feared. They didn't expect me to overcome and achieve success. They expected me to simply get by and join the ranks of the working poor in our nation and in our cities. They expected that I would operate on the margins of our society and that my children would do the same.

I was a conscientious teen and thought about these things, and it made me more resolute to be one of the kids the agency showcased to White people who gave money. Most people in my life didn't care that I was in foster care and had a rough life. Given that the first fifteen years of my life had followed the grim statistics laid out for me, how could I prove the experts wrong? How could I show

A lot of people didn't expect me to do anything different than what my parents had done, just as I feared. They didn't expect me to overcome and achieve success.

my younger brother and sister that we could make it if we tried really hard? How could I show them that we could do and be anything we wanted to do and be in life?

These were the ideas I pondered, inspired after the acquisition of "life skills." Life skills weren't just crucial for practical use; they held significance as they represented a lower societal status many thought I'd be confined to due to my lack of family and upbringing. During my brief year or more at Annie Malone, I had outgrown the facility that had worked to give me structure and some good experiences. The agency did its best to equip me with a *survivor's* toolkit. However, I wanted the *thriver's* toolkit.

I realized that for most of my life, I had played it safe. Prior to Annie Malone, playing it safe where life and death decisions were present often meant the opposite of what mainstream America teaches about how to operate in a violent society. A desire for self-preservation leads you to strike first and hardest. In a predatory environment, you must exert more energy to determine when, where, and with whom to be vulnerable. Thinking back, I took a risk by letting the kid in the alley get up instead of hitting him with that brick. It was a public demonstration of vulnerability that I wasn't accustomed to. The irony is that playing it safe will ensure you live a predictable life. For me, that predictable life was prison or death or some other dead-end circumstance that would exercise control over me.

We must risk something, I thought. So many of us refuse to take risks because we don't want to experience the emotional deflation that comes from failure. This fear forces us to limit our potential by keeping us in emotional and psychological safety zones. Playing it safe will ensure you have a predictable life, and if you don't have anything, you'll have more of the same—absolutely nothing. I had to think like a normal person, a person who wasn't always on edge, always running hot, and take a measured risk.

Taking measured risks is energizing and creates a flywheel that stretches you even more, one risk at a time, in pursuit of your goals. Taking measured risks is about believing in yourself, the quality of your execution, and, if you fail or succeed, the velocity of your rebound or compound. To rebound is to get up quickly and try again. To compound is to seize on the success, build on that effort, and achieve even more. It's kind of like compound interest.

We learn as kids through the natural course of development to take small steps—like crawling, pulling up, and ultimately walking—which lead to bigger rewards and independence. Those small steps create muscle memory and positive reinforcement if we are in a functioning environment.

In a dysfunctional environment, we learn to take fight-or-flight risks. Fear prompted the first big, measured risk that I recall—I told my mother that I was being sexually abused. I was five years old and feared he would kill me and harm my siblings like he said he would. I had nightmares about what was happening to me and what would happen to us. My vivid imagination took me to horrible places and forced this normal fight or flight response. I chose to fight. I needed to choose to fight again.

During my sophomore year, I realized that I didn't have a Plan B. I had no fallback plan. No parents, no permanent support. I learned in the life skills courses that I would age out once I turned eighteen. If you're in school, the state will continue to support you, but I needed a plan.

To flourish means to thrive. It means to be fulfilled and have a sense of purpose. It would be a while before achievement and flourishing were on my radar. It would be a while before I considered that I needed people to ultimately achieve my goals, feed my hunger, and help me connect to opportunities—but I would get there. I eventually realized that my approach to aggression had to acknowledge my need for community and connection with others, as well as my responsibility in regulating my emotions. This understanding is crucial for fostering a community that supports one another and building a future characterized by prosperity for all.

We tend to stay emotionally connected to relationships we've outgrown because they are familiar, even in their dysfunction. My relationship with my mother should have been more than familiar; it should have been covenantal. I've learned that few meaningful relationships function for a lifetime, so you must be intentional about pruning and curating mutually beneficial relationships with the right people who have the right mindset and who are deserving of your trust, your time, and your attention right now.

Though I can't say I'm close to many, I have mastered the art of functional relationships. Functional relationships are those that work for you, where mutual benefit exists. My wife and kids provide me with purpose; I provide them with love and security. My work relationships offer a path to achieving more than I can alone; in return, I provide avenues for them to reach their potential and shared prosperity. Those who mentor or sponsor me offer advice and access, while I bring a sponge-like curiosity, a teachable spirit, and a desire to succeed. I am a conduit, and I pass on what I learn with due credit. I am eager to share who has taught me what and provided a platform, mentoring, or sponsorship because none of us truly succeed alone.

We must also know when we've exhausted the possibilities in our existing relationships. This generally becomes evident when you stop growing. As a young person, I subscribed to the belief that familiarity breeds contempt. This forced a guarding of my heart and head that is still somewhat present today. Familiarity only breeds contempt if you're outgrowing the person or persons in your network. Familiarity breeds contempt if you allow people to exalt you. Then, the closer they get, they realize you're just a man or you're just a woman, and you're subject to the same challenges and struggles of all people.

Knowing when to exit a relationship is as important as entering. You don't have to be overly dramatic about sunsetting most relationships. Chances are when you stop showing up, it's a sign that you're pruning. When you stop showing up, just view it as a shift of energy toward more fruitful relationships. And just because you prune, it doesn't mean that relationship will never be meaningful again.

Functional relationships—even those that are true friendships that provide emotional security—are few. By taking stock of our relationships, we can get a clearer sense of those who are helping us achieve our goals and those who are not. It's helpful to assign purposes to relationships and think about mutual exchange and value creation to determine if the relationship is balanced over time. If you're extracting from me in every season of life, then that relationship is likely not healthy for either of us. Having functional relationships also means that there's no mandate to stay emotionally connected to dysfunctional relationships, even if it's with family members. Dysfunctional relationships create barriers to our growth. By focusing on a few relationships that are high impact, we can prioritize our time and be more focused. I needed to focus and move past the safety of the Annie Malone relationship.

It was as clear as day that I needed to get on a path to stop taking orders and develop the muscle to care for myself. I needed to take more control over my life. I needed more freedom. There was only a little time before I'd officially be on my own, so I acted like it. I grew up and intended to establish new relationships to make my mark on the world—like Annie Malone, the entrepreneur and business leader; like The Ville neighborhood, once home to Black excellence; like those corporate board members and volunteers who invested so much of their time to ensure my basic needs were met.

I needed a different environment and didn't want to wait to get into the Independent Living Program. I was now seventeen and motivated to move on and chase my excellence. So, I did. I moved on and was inspired to make my mark, knowing God had a plan for my life. The darkness of my childhood was giving way to a lighted path.

NEVER STRAY

I struggle along the way
but my vision
shall never stray
the success that I desire
is beyond what man can make

You judge my character
without knowing my soul
the relationship that I share
with my God
only He and I know

I say my God
cause that's how I think
each bond with He
is truly special
and unique

I'm queried along my walk
of my spiritual line
what denomination
do I dedicate my time

I'm dedicated to God
and being the best that I can be
under the circumstances
that has been placed upon me

Each day builds upon the last
it creates a foundation of hope
That through the most beneficent
I'll survive the past

The future it seems so crystal clear
if I stay steadfast in my beliefs
set goals, derive objectives
be mindful of the barriers that
I know will be erected

Take steps to actualize my goals
in light of the fear
of failing or falling near
and having my deficits exposed
I realize that I am only human
And I'll make some mistakes
But I'll learn and reengineer my approach
As the days pass away
Rest assured that my vision
Shall never go astray.

CHAPTER 5

*"When I dare to be powerful, to use my strength in the service
of my vision, then it becomes less and less important
whether I am afraid."*

—Audre Lorde

As a kid, so much had been planted in me to nurture my uncertainty and passivity. I was a passive young man for the longest time because I knew deep down that I was capable of great aggression. I didn't know how to want something without wanting it aggressively. My life was an emotional mess, and I never wanted to lose my emotional control, so I focused on what was immediately in front of me. I stayed out of trouble and did everything I could to avoid conflict. Any conflict, including internal, I believed, would take more from me than I'd gain.

By the time I was old enough to know better, I would always course-correct if I did or said anything that crossed the line, particularly with adults who showed a genuine interest in me.

When asked about any serious futuristic matter, a gloom would come over me because it pointed to a larger issue: I didn't have a plan. I was grim and serious-minded because I wanted it but didn't know how to pursue it. When it came to the really serious things, I was often elusive.

In addition to my unassertiveness and internal conflicts, I was also a conformist during my youth. I didn't want to do anything that was unconventional. I didn't take risks that would put me outside the mainstream for fear that the few trusting adults I had in my life—teachers, counselors, priests, nuns—would disapprove. I generally followed the rules and did what was expected. I often joked that if you entrusted me with your car keys to run an errand to the store, even as a seventeen-year-old boy curious about girls, I would reliably travel directly from point A to point B. I doubt many boys my age would show such discipline, but for me, it was necessary to stay safe and avoid trouble.

As I entered young adulthood, my desire for independence grew stronger. I wanted to break free from the expectations and limitations set by others. I craved the freedom to make my own choices and pursue my own passions without fear of judgment or disapproval. It was time to nurture a vision for my future. Even in my uncertainty, I spent time both casting vision to inspire others to believe in my potential and meditating on that vision to ensure it aligned with my deeper values and goals.

IN THE MIDDLE OF MY SOPHOMORE YEAR at the Academy of Math and Science, I transitioned from the Annie Malone Children's Home to the Emergency Children's Home (ECHO) at 3033 North Euclid, just 1.5 miles away. Operating under the Disciples of Christ Church, ECHO served as both a ministry and provider of social services, marking an ideal next chapter in my life. As we approached, the thought *Freedom at last!* crossed my mind.

I vividly remember the moment my case worker informed me about the move.

"Hello, Orvin," she began.

"Yes," I replied, already sensing the purpose of her call, filled with an indescribable sense of excitement. ECHO promised a more liberating environment and hinted at the possibility of having a semblance of normal teenage life.

"You've been accepted," she said. Words can't quite explain what I felt. Those words—"You have been accepted"—lingered long in my mind.

I was accepted! I thought.

In ECHO's Independent Living Program, the residence usually hosted between four and eight occupants, and it created a dynamic and ever-changing environment. Most residents, unlike me, had moved there from ECHO's residential program. The house we were now in was modest, and it reminded me of the one I shared with Shirley, although it appeared smaller because I'd grown. It was a humble house with two rooms upstairs, each outfitted with four beds, and it embodied a simplicity that held the potential for a new beginning.

Like the Annie Malone Children's Home, ECHO had a house parent, Mr. Gerald. He was an older gentleman with keloids on his face like Shirley. His job was to keep tabs on us and all the activity in the home. Mr. Gerald drove an old, beat-up red station wagon that we used to shop for food for the house.

The kitchen and living room were on the first floor, and that's where we had group therapy. The kitchen was adjacent to a door that opened to the parking lot, and it provided a view of the sprawling campus. The dorms for girls and boys in the residential side and the offices were on the other side of the campus. We had an outdoor basketball court and an indoor gym. I spent a lot of time on the court trying, without success, to get better.

Mr. Pratt, an old White guy, oversaw ECHO, serving as its chief executive officer. There was also Mr. Calhoun, who always sported a nicely cut mini-afro and wore a suit. He, too, was an executive. I believe he was over operations, serving as Mr. Pratt's second in command. He was also older but not as old as Mr. Pratt. Mr. Calhoun was tall. *Surely*, I thought, *he played some basketball in his day.*

Mr. Calhoun would always say, "How are you today, young man?" in a firm but authentic way when we crossed paths. He was more of a fatherly figure on campus than any other worker.

I lived in a house with other young men. We grocery-shopped, cooked, and did other chores to keep the house functioning. Most everyone worked outside jobs. We were out of the house most weekdays and came home to eat, do chores, and go to sleep. I did my homework either directly after school, while on breaks during work, or on the bus going back to ECHO.

They were sticklers for the rules at ECHO. If you were going to miss curfew, you needed to call. I never missed curfew. As a young person, much of my behavior was driven by my desire to fit in and meet the expectations of authority figures. I believed my survival depended on maintaining control, which often meant self-denial. This led me to blame myself for any disruptions in life, feeling I needed to "be good." My survival was also tied to my ability to punish myself; sometimes, this punishment was as simple as denying myself social interaction. I didn't default to fun.

I lived in a house with other young men. We grocery-shopped, cooked, and did other chores to keep the house functioning. Most everyone worked outside jobs.

I liked girls, but I avoided being with them because it wasn't acceptable to the church or the adults in my life. Plus, the likely outcome of being with a girl—pregnancy and father-hood—wasn't feasible for me since I had nothing.

I met Sabrina during my junior year in high school when I was eighteen years old. She was a freshman and was fifteen years old. I was very conscious of the fact that, due to my December birthday, I was almost always the oldest person in my class, which forced me to start school late—and, of course, because I was held back in second grade. Sabrina had three sisters and a mom. They lived in a two-family flat in South Saint Louis, not too far from where I worked at the Schnucks Market on Grand and Gravois.

I fell hard for her. It wasn't like that early feeling I had with Angel, one of the first girls I ever noticed. This was different. Sabrina was smart, funny, quiet, introverted, and beautiful. She was as bright as sunshine (remember Ralph's wife from my time at Shirley's). Sabrina had disarming hazel eyes and a com-pelling spirit of determination, and she captured something inside me. We both attended Gateway Institute of Technology (Gateway Tech), and I first noticed her after school when I was taking the same bus to work.

Sabrina and I dated for about a year; we spent significant time together, sharing a lot of firsts, seconds, and thirds. I often told her that I loved her and could see us together in the future. On Saturdays, I got off work at 4:00 p.m. or 5:00 p.m. after an eight-hour shift, where I thought of her each moment—you know, real love. After that, I would go over to Sabrina's place and would stay until 9:00 p.m. or 10:00 p.m., where we talked about life, took walks, napped, and did what-ever. I never wanted to leave when it was time to take the last bus back to North Saint Louis to ECHO.

I cared deeply for her, so much so that I felt compelled to pull back during my senior year. I feared getting too entangled in the relationship, possibly losing sight of my goal—college. Unfortunately, the timing of our connection worked against us. I was unsure how to navigate such intense emotions, so my easiest recourse was to withdraw. This decision inadvertently opened the door for other guys to step in. I wasn't pleased with the knucklehead she ended up with after me; she got married quickly, but I no longer had a say in her life.

After Sabrina, I became a serial dater. I vowed not to date anyone longer than six months so I wouldn't "catch feelings." During my senior year, a girl I was dating teased me and said I was afraid of, well, you know, sex. She blurted this out at school in front of our friends.

She said, "Orvin had a chance to get some this weekend, and he didn't take it." I was so embarrassed, but she got a kick out of it, poking me and laughing while others hung on to her every word. I think she was trying to fit in because the cool kids or the in-crowd were all presumably "doing it." I wasn't certain that she had ever done it. But she was right; she had made overtures, and I may have had a chance with her. It wasn't that I was afraid; I just didn't want to disappoint her parents, who'd been so kind to this sewer kid. Her dad had asked me point blank, "Are you and Stephanie having sex?"

"No, sir," I said.

I was determined to keep it that way, not wanting to step over the line, because I'd grown to respect her mom and dad. They were good people. I spent a lot of time with Stephanie and her parents and was so impressed with their two-parent family. They lived near where I lived at ECHO in one of the newly built townhomes that had a gate all around them. I used to pass by this place but never went in because of the huge gate surrounding it. *I know rich people live there,* I thought. I knew they had to be rich, or at least middle class, because this was one of the first new developments I'd seen in all my years of living in North City.

This was also when Mr. Kindle, Stephanie's dad, began asking me about college. I didn't know for sure if I wanted to go, but the seed for college had been planted. He and his wife took great interest in my future prospects, and they regularly asked me about my plans as I often found myself in their company, spending time with Stephanie and talking to them about life. Stephanie was certain that her next step was college because she was raised in an environment where it was the expectation. I don't know for certain what Mr. and Mrs. Kindle did for a living—he was maybe an engineer—but they lived well and treated me kindly. They were good people.

I often lay on their yellow print couch alongside Stephanie. She was part girlfriend, part counselor, always wondering what was going on with me. Fun and in tune with my rhythm, she would ask when I sunk into myself, "What's wrong, Orvin?" I often heard this same question from adults.

"Nothing," I would say.

People always assumed there was more going on with me than I let on, and they were right. Whether with the Kindles or anyone else, I was trying to overcome this inner tug-of-war. I was trying to find faith in my abilities in the midst of people who seemed certain, and to be more sure of who I was as a growing boy. In addition to lacking confidence in my ability to achieve greatly, I struggled with my outward appearance, which was evident in my tendency to downgrade myself. *You are not handsome*, I would customarily remind myself, and I rarely found refuge from these dejecting thoughts.

More than anyone during this period, Stephanie would tell me I was handsome. She would write notes, "To my handsome, good-looking friend, who I hope to soon become more than friends."

I always struggled with what to do with this. Stephanie, of course, was a beautiful girl inside and out. *Why does she think I'm handsome?* I thought.

As I reflect on my relationships with Sabrina and Stephanie, my state of mind at the time led me to a realization. Sabrina, my first high school sweetheart, although I deeply cared for her, wasn't the one to spend my life with. We were too early, too young. I didn't want us to become a distraction for each other by connecting so deeply so early in our lives.

The possibility of a future with Stephanie also seemed a stretch for the same reason and more. It was too early and given her middle-class background and the culturally rich and diverse environment she represented, signified by the Buddha images in her home and her extensive travel experiences—she was destined to succeed. She was what friends would say, "out of my league." And besides, I needed more than to just be in love.

I was still afraid of making mistakes, like becoming a young parent or taking big relationship risks, so I restricted my behavior and feelings to what felt safe and acceptable. Neither Stephanie nor Sabrina felt safe, as I could have easily lost myself. I was also afraid of appearing unconventional by declaring my love as a teenager and committing to one person. Some high school couples were on this path, but it scared me.

I had a healthy dose of self-doubt, likely more than the average teen during this period. I had a deflated sense of self-esteem, which actually forced me to overcompensate with an unflinching work ethic. Riding shotgun through most of my high school relationships was Lamar, my best friend from the Academy of Math and Science. During this period, I dove deeper into my writing, drew closer to the Church, and began to explore an aspect of my identity that seemed beyond the Church's comprehension—the identity of a Black male.

MY YOUNGER BROTHER WAS AT ECHO when I arrived. I saw him occasionally, usually in the gym. He hung out with kids who I felt were a bit rough: Earnest Blackwell, Marcus (a kid who stood out because I had a crush on his girlfriend early in my time at ECHO), and others. Earnest was a standout football player, and a few years later, we ended up in the same college dorm. During those college years, Earnest embraced me like a brother.

In our freshman year, he offered, "If you ever need a car stereo system, I can hook you up."

Sadly, Earnest passed away at age twenty-nine after allegedly shooting his stepdaughter and attacking his neighbors. He died following a struggle with the police. He'd been tazed and subdued with drugs.

When I wasn't playing basketball or working, I was at Lamar's house, penning rhymes. During this period, I started to discover my identity, and music was another outlet for exploration and expression. I had always been a writer, and since rap was popular at the time, I translated my thoughts into rhymes and took part in talent shows across North Saint Louis. My social circle was mainly made up of individuals from school, ECHO, or the foster care system.

Lamar lived with his grandmother up the street from ECHO, and his proximity to my group home fostered our deep friendship. We both played basketball for a while, were very socially conscious, and enjoyed being super silly with each other. We hung out after school or on the weekends when there were no other commitments.

It wasn't uncommon for Lamar to say in a frustrated but joking manner, "I will slap the shit out of you."

To which I would say, "I dare you." Sure enough, he would slap the shit out of me and run away while I chased him, both of us laughing hysterically. We loved to dare each other to see who could be the most egregious. We went back and forth with these kinds of antics, and it was all in good fun. I trusted Lamar, and we established a rap group called Young Black Intelligence (YBI).

We were a group of kids whose development could have been arrested, but we were finding ways to channel our energies by hanging out, writing, and practicing in Lamar's grandmother's basement. Another older guy in the neighborhood had a makeshift recording studio in his basement, and the walls were lined with foam to control the sound. This is where Lamar, his cousin, E-Money, and I recorded several songs. YBI was important because, at the time, there was a proliferation of negative images in the media, music, and popular culture—about Black boys and men in particular—and this negative depiction didn't represent us. YBI focused mostly on uplifting music. One of our first recordings, "Caged Bird," likely inspired by Maya Angelou's classic poem, was generally expressive about how we felt at times—*caged* in our community. After moving out of ECHO, my relationship with Lamar started deteriorating.

I no longer maintain any of my childhood relationships. I've been disconnected in a real sense from my past since I graduated high school. Most of my memories of childhood are difficult, and thus, these relationships are a constant reminder of the pain and lack. Not to mention that life takes people in different directions based on wants, needs, aspirations, state of mind—and social networks.

My life had been one trauma after the next, and I didn't learn how to navigate through problems like most kids do. In a typical family, when kids make mistakes, they have something to fall back on—parents who help them learn and make better choices. I didn't have any of

I no longer maintain any of my childhood relationships. I've been disconnected in a real sense from my past since I graduated high school.

that. Like Annie Malone, I didn't have a pedigree, inheritance, or even parents. I relied on observing the people and situations around me and learning from them.

What I saw taught me that residential facilities like the Annie Malone Children's Home and ECHO are, by necessity, based on a law of averages. They must do the greatest good for the greatest number of kids facing tremendous challenges. "Success" in these settings means keeping young people productive and alive until they're ready to age out of the system.

According to the Annie E. Casey Foundation, about 20,000 young people age out of the foster care system annually and are left to fend for themselves. When kids face conditions like what I experienced, they encounter a set of expectations that institutions anticipate from them. They may conform to those expectations, turning them into a self-fulfilling prophecy like "Oh, this is all most people think I can do? OK, that's all I'll try." Fortunately, my exposure to things like the Saint Louis University basketball team and the outings with the Annie Malone Children's Home made me realize that I aspired for more.

There was a guy who used to live at ECHO and went to Lincoln University, an HBCU in Jefferson City, Missouri, after high school. He came back during school breaks in a big black car with rims. I thought that was so cool. He stayed at ECHO when he was in town because he didn't have parents or other resources to live with. The more I saw him, the more I could see myself as a college student someday.

At the end of my junior year, a woman named Joyce—the same woman who allowed my older brother to live with her—took me in, which gave me a chance to live in a single-family home in the community. My older brother was now headed to college on a football scholarship, so she gave me a shot at living in a more typical family setting before I was officially launched into adulthood. I was beyond thrilled.

Joyce was a single mom who worked at the post office. She got up every day, no matter how she felt, and went to work. She didn't ask much of me except to clean up after myself and do well in school. That year, she allowed me to take the driver's test in her car, and I got my license. Having a driver's license was a newfound independence. On most Friday nights, she let me borrow her car to go on a date or to pick a friend up and bring her back to the house to hang out. Joyce was really laid back and was a lot of fun. She would always say, "Boys will be boys."

Her adult son Deontre and nephew Steve, who also happened to be my godfather, lived with her for a while and had profound influences on me. I learned how to be more confident around the ladies by watching Steve, and I smoked my first joint with these guys. When my oldest brother Antwon found out, he was really upset.

He shouted, "What the heck are you doing?" as he watched me take a puff of the joint and pass it on.

Deontre was probably the most conscientious Black man I knew at the time. He had fully mature locks, smoked reefer all the time, and philosophized about everything. Through him, I learned there were alternative belief systems, like the belief that 144,000 people would go to heaven. I didn't quite understand this, but I did understand that Deontre was unapologetically for lifting up Black people.

During my time with Joyce, I reconnected with Djaun, my former houseparent at the Annie Malone Children's Home, who'd gone on to become a director at the YMCA. After one night of basketball at the YMCA, where he allowed me free access to keep me off the streets, Djuan asked if I wanted to join a march "to take back our streets." I said, "Sure." So, for a few Saturday nights, we convened at a mosque and marched the streets, chanting in solidarity and vowing to take our streets back from the gang members and drug dealers. The group we were a part of was called the Fruit of Islam, which is the security arm of the Nation of Islam.

I'd been exposed to Islam a bit by Deontre but wasn't immersed in its teachings. To learn more, I purchased the 1965 book *A Message to the Black Man* by Elijah Muhammad and began to study it. The most important lesson I learned from marching the streets and reading the book was that my life as a Black man had value and purpose, and I had a right to be self-determined. In my senior picture, I was wearing denim jeans, a Tommy Hilfiger shirt, rocking Timberland boots, and, of course, holding the book *A Message to the Black Man,* which was my message to the world that couldn't stand my existence that I, too, wanted to be unapologetically Black. My consciousness was clearly shifting.

Living with Joyce during my senior year was a dream come true, but I knew it wasn't a long-term plan. I needed other alternatives. I started to survey my options for what life would hold after I aged out of the foster care system. No matter the direction, it would be a challenge. My first option was to simply get a job. However, I'd seen a lot of people who just got jobs, lived for that paycheck, and years later still just had a job. As much as I liked having money, I knew that wasn't me. The military was another option. I'd been in the Air Force ROTC at Gateway Tech, but my entire life was regulated, and I didn't want anybody else to have that much control over me anymore. Finally, there was college. Even through my limited experience, I'd seen that education opened doors. So that's where I set my sights.

Finally, there was college. Even through my limited experience, I'd seen that education opened doors. So that's where I set my sights.

I worked hard the last year and a half of high school to improve my grades. I didn't realize that my earlier grades carried more weight toward my average. Nonetheless, I stayed focused and decided to apply to one school, the University of Missouri-Columbia.

College would be a stretch for me, both academically and financially. I was a below-average student and not really college material. I got a fifteen on my ACT test, and every intelligence test I'd ever taken said I was below average in quantitative intelligence and critical thinking. Even worse, some of my social workers doubted my ability to succeed. To them, I was just another child of a welfare mom, a ward of the state, and a loner with no models of success. I'd rarely seen anyone make it out of my environment and achieve over time. As a result, I sometimes doubted my ability to succeed.

However, I had drive and the ability to sell my vision. When I finally worked up the courage, I went to Mr. Calhoun and Mrs. Reeves, the powerful new head of ECHO. It was the first time I saw a pair of Black leaders leading an organization, and I shared my vision with them.

"College is my only option," I said. Not knowing exactly what it meant, but only what it felt like, I added, "I want to help people like me."

They encouraged me by saying, "I believe you can do it."

I begged the University of Missouri-Columbia (Mizzou) to let me in. They reminded me that I hadn't tested well and had average grades.

"Perhaps you're better suited for community college," they suggested.

I thought community college was fine for some kids. However, to me, it was like an extension of high school, and I knew if I stayed in Saint Louis, there were too many traps that I could get caught in—the old neighborhood, old friends who weren't doing anything new, old girls, who were probably doing everyone old and new. I just couldn't risk it. I knew deep down that I needed to be in a different environment. I needed to be in an environment, quite frankly, that would expose me to new thoughts that would stretch me. So, I persisted and didn't accept no for an answer from Mizzou.

After weeks of me badgering the university, they finally told me about a program that required below-average students like me to take a college-level math and English course during the summer at the University of Missouri-Saint Louis (UMSL) as a prerequisite for entering Mizzou. If I received a grade of B or better, I'd be allowed into the university on academic probation. I shared the news with Mr. Calhoun because the next barrier was that I needed $600 for the classes. I didn't have that kind of money, and Joyce certainly didn't have it. I didn't even bother to ask her because I thought, *She's being generous enough simply allowing me to stay in her home and ensuring I eat.*

After a couple of weeks, Mr. Calhoun and Mrs. Reeves called me into the office to give me the news.

"We found a sponsor and have secured $600 for you to take the classes this summer," they said.

I was elated because this was my last barrier, aside from trying to figure out how to get to the campus daily during the summer. As I walked off the ECHO campus that day, I thought to myself, *OK, this is real. Now, don't fuck it up. You have to focus.*

UMSL was in North Saint Louis County. In preparation for attending, I visited the campus. It was exhilarating, unlike any other place I'd been, filled with possibilities. I got a bus pass and took it daily to UMSL, arriving as early as possible to take in the campus and study. Sometimes after class, I would go to Washington University, which I was exposed to through my high school German class, to study—because it made me feel smarter. College was a different world. Both classes, Math and English, seemed larger than I was used to in high school. I sat up front and tried to stay focused. English came more naturally to me than College Algebra.

Algebra was akin to a foreign language that I just didn't seem to get. It was so abstract, where numbers were represented by symbols. *I don't know why this shit has to be this difficult*, I thought. English was pretty straightforward—do this research, write this paper, take a position in the paper, and watch your grammar and sentence structure. You know, normal stuff. I didn't realize then that numbers also tell stories.

As the summer went on, panic and anxiety set in. The pressure to figure out an alternative path had intensified. What was I going to do about this algebra class? I talked to an advisor, who encouraged me to talk to the instructor, who wasn't very encouraging about my prospects.

"Perhaps you should consider community college," he said.

Boy, I thought, *the road to achieving anything is difficult.* I wasn't having it. I didn't want to go to community college. I had set my mind on Mizzou and needed to figure out how to get there.

During one discussion, our instructor said, "Exceptional students opted early in the summer to test out of the math class."

That's it, I thought. In my class, of course, were students like me who simply didn't apply themselves in high school and were in the same boat I was in. I truly was a deficient traditional learner with an IQ of seventy (one hundred was average) and a faulty foundation for math. After inquiring further, I learned that *anybody* could take the exam to test out of algebra at any point, up to the final class.

I decided I could only succeed by testing out of the course. I learned there were no restrictions on how many times you could take the exam. I pumped myself up by developing a strategy I believed could help me win—the strategy by memory.

Through the years, I'd been able to remember lots of rap songs that I'd written and performed, and I remembered the pattern of Shirley's hands on the keypad to turn off the alarm. I remembered all the words of defeat that I'd heard. I remembered all the abuse; in fact, sometimes, these memories became more vivid at night. Strategy by memory was my only shot. I needed to memorize all the questions on the test and practice them to ultimately pass so I could move on to the University of Missouri-Columbia. *This is life or death,* I thought.

After taking the test the third time, I realized there were variations of the test. Point noted. I took the test six times, and after each time, I started writing down everything I could remember as soon as I left the room. Literally, I would rush out of the room, say "Thank you" as I handed my sheet in, and move quickly out the glass door to sit on the ledge. I wrote feverishly about everything I could remember from the test. From those notes, I put together a practical study guide and reconstructed the types of equations I'd be asked to solve. As I studied the notes, I started noticing patterns and relationships. I did my best to memorize the facts of these patterns and relationships, and I practiced over and over. On the sixth time, I handed in my test and moved a little more slowly because I believed I had nailed it.

I believe that achievement comes through pushing yourself harder than the next person.
Being smart does not equal success.

I did! I nailed it! I passed! I was going to college. However, as important as it was to pass that math class, the more important thing was what I learned about myself.

Several times as I've moved through my career, potential employers have given me aptitude tests. They always say the same thing: below average in quantitative skills but outstanding in the ability to achieve. I believe that achievement comes through pushing yourself harder than the next person. Being smart does not equal success. I knew a lot of smart people in high school, but they often ended up being those who just got jobs. Achievement comes from hard work. Even today, sometimes, when I'm giving a speech, I make myself sit down and memorize it, just like I memorized those math tests. My love of language and experience rapping helped; being aware of pitch and cadence is the key to memorization. However, in the end, you need more than tricks like that to succeed. You need discipline, focus, and persistence.

My decision to go to college also helped me understand the connection between courage and vulnerability. It took courage to say, "I'm going to college," but the vulnerability was, "I might fail." To succeed, you have to give yourself a pep talk and say, "I'm going to do it scared; I'm going to do it anyway."

Imagine if Annie Malone had given up because she listened to the people who told her, "You can't succeed! You're a woman. You're Black. You don't have a pedigree." There would have been no Poro Beauty Products, Poro College, or Annie Malone Children's Home. Instead, she had a vision and kept going.

I did, too.

PEACE WITHIN ME

Here I stand
All grown into a man
Eagerly awaiting God's great big plan
Wondering how things would have been
had your life not come to such a tragic end

Thinking back it still doesn't make sense
though I never felt your unconditional love
the pain was still immense

There are so many things that I want to say
As I lie here and reflect on that catastrophic day

The precipitating events that culminated in your death
consumed your every move
till you exhaled your very last breath

You injected your veins with poison
to further escape your reality you drank in excess
You prostituted your body in search of money and love
which you never did find or get

You allowed many invasions to take place within our home
I looked at you as my security above all and yet
you were always gone

You placed all others before me
How many ways did this manifest
You were naïve to the motives
of a live-in guest
as he crushed my childhood innocence

You neglected to hear my cries
You neglected to see my tears
You neglected to tell me
that you loved me
Even if it wasn't sincere

You caused me to experience that kind of hurt
that doesn't cure so easily
It's taken me years to get to this point
But now I've found
peace within me and I forgive you.

CHAPTER 6

"When you have mastered numbers, you will in fact no longer be reading numbers, any more than you read words when reading books. You will be reading meanings."

—*W.E.B. DuBois*

It was hard to process that I'd gotten into college. However, I had a vision and kept moving toward it.

"How does it feel?" I was often asked.

"It feels great. I'm so proud," I would say.

And this was true. I did feel great, and I was proud that I'd set my mind to a very difficult task and accomplished it. However, I also felt like a fraud, and I was afraid. Actually, I was terrified. I had so many unanswered questions in my mind. *What if I didn't have more to give?* I thought. *What if miraculously testing out of a class that I was failing was my last move?* I wondered. *What if I can't outsmart the system, or even more, what if I'm just not good enough to complete college-level work?*

There would be no more convenient explanations about why I was behind in life—poverty, substandard education, death of mom, absent dad, abuse, and foster care. I thought

I'd earned a chance that many didn't get, and the truth was that I believed—based on my mental conditioning—that there was a high probability that I would default on that chance. It was a heavy burden I harbored. During my senior year, when the other kids talked about where they were going to college, I couldn't say with any confidence that I was *permanently* college bound. I only knew I'd been accepted into a summer program to take two college-level courses: college English and remedial Algebra.

Mizzou heavily recruited Black students in 1994 and offered a full-ride African American scholarship. This was nearly forty-five years after Mizzou admitted its first Black students due to a lawsuit from Lloyd Gaines, an aspiring law student who was aided by the National Advancement of Colored People (NAACP) to get accepted into Mizzou's all-White law school. It was forty years after the landmark Topeka v. Board of Education Supreme Court case of 1954 that struck down "separate but equal" as the law of the land. Still struggling with diversity, in 1994, the largest cohort of Black students in Mizzou's history, about six hundred strong, was recruited to a campus population of around 20,000.

Many of my friends were going to other colleges. My good friend Hubert, with whom I played basketball and hung out socially at his mother's large home in the city, was bound for Saint Louis University (SLU), where I interned. SLU was a tough school to get into. *Hubert was pretty good in math,* I remembered. The year before, Janine, a good friend and daughter of my junior varsity basketball coach, went to Purdue University in Lafayette, Indiana. I thought that was cool. I thought it must be something to have the confidence to go all the way to Indiana.

"Purdue is only four hours away," she said, but that seemed like a whole world away to me. My best friend, Lamar, decided to attend the historically Black college, Lane College, in

Jackson, Tennessee. Even with all my Black consciousness, I didn't know much about Historically Black Colleges and Universities (HBCUs). This was when I came to understand that Black and White schools had official designations. According to the National Center for Education Statistics, The US Department of Education defines an HBCU as ". . . any historically Black college or university that was established prior to 1964, whose principal mission was, and is, the education of Black Americans, and that is accredited by a nationally recognized accrediting agency. . ." The US Department of Education defines a Predominantly White Institution (PWI) as a university that has 50 percent or more enrollment from White students. It is also used to refer to any university that is deemed "historically White."

My address had changed so many times throughout childhood and high school, which always meant significant change. I started life near 5300 Wabada, where mom died; moved to the 2800 block of Semple, where Shirley had her stroke; then was sent to 2600 Annie Malone Drive and 3033 North Euclid, where I lived in orphanages before I moved in with Joyce. However, the most dramatic change was moving to South Ninth Street, the official address for the University of Missouri-Columbia, where I enrolled in college.

. . . I traveled to Columbia, Missouri, to start my college education. It was the first time I'd been out of the city of Saint Louis or East Saint Louis since I was nine.

After finally overcoming my summer hurdle of remedial classes and successfully petitioning to go to Mizzou, I traveled to Columbia, Missouri, to start my college education. It was the first time I'd been out of the city of Saint Louis or East Saint Louis since I was nine. I'd never seen the acres of farmland, small towns, or middle-of-nowhere gas stations that dotted the ninety-minute drive west along I-70 to Columbia. When I got to town, the campus was alive with activity—young adults were all over the place, joking around and laughing as they unloaded their parents' cars and U-Hauls packed full of clothes, TVs, stereos, food, everything.

Mizzou, and more generally Columbia, was the whitest place I'd ever seen. *Mizzou is definitely a PWI,* I thought as I took it all in. It was intimidating, to say the least. White people, who seemingly had it all, were everywhere. I had to battle my thoughts even more in their presence because, in my world, I had been falsely convinced they were the standard of excellence.

My belongings were meager compared to theirs, and I felt alone. So, I called Shirley's sister, Brenda, the only person I knew in town. I'd always looked up to Brenda and her husband, Charles. They seemed like they had it all together. It hadn't been their fault that Shirley preferred their kids, Deanna and Russ, over us, and I still had good memories of those magic days when they would come to visit, and the house would seem to lift off its foundation. Brenda always had positive energy. When she pulled up, I could see her big smile and the prominent gap in her teeth as I stepped out of the dorm and went to the pickup spot.

Reaching over the seat as I entered, she hugged me, oozing pride, stating, "I am so glad to see you."

I settled into the car with mixed emotions. I was definitely excited to see her, but I was also in a dark mood because I hadn't had a chance to see her more often when I was growing up. As our car made its way to Walmart, I wondered what my life would have been like if she had been the sister who took the four of us in instead of Shirley.

I didn't know what to expect. I wondered if we would pick out things, and while standing at the checkout register, Brenda would disappear. Instead, she loaded my cart with snacks and supplies. She didn't disappear but whipped out her credit card to cover the bill. I couldn't help but look up to her with gratitude. It was one of the nicest things anyone had ever done for me. She dropped me off, and I made several trips from the car to my dorm room. I hugged Brenda once more as I retrieved the last load, looked up at the stars, and thought, *This was a very good day filled with kindness.*

Occasionally, I would see my cousin, Russ—Brenda's son—in the gym hooping. He was just another cat who didn't attend the university but came to the yard to hoop and party. We had no connection. I only saw Brenda one more time during my time in Columbia, which reinforced my early trauma that I had no family, no foundation, and no fallback plan. College was my shot and my shot alone.

Over the weekend, I settled into my dorm and explored the campus. One evening, I overheard some guys outside who were rapping and laughing. I thought, *Rappers at Mizzou—no way!* I went downstairs and out the door to meet a group that included J-Scott.

Years later, we pledged the same fraternity, Alpha Phi Alpha. After high school, I vowed that if I was going to be successful in college, I needed to be focused. I couldn't commit the time that I'd once invested in making music, so, despite the energizing experience of witnessing rappers on campus, I disengaged from that group as quickly as I had engaged.

I walked the campus and observed the White Greek row near my dorm and across the street from the running tracks at Rothwell Gym. White Greeks partied hard that weekend and most every weekend. I found myself connecting with freshmen on a basketball court late at night, hooping. This was cool because it reminded me a bit of the outdoor court at the Annie Malone Children's Home and ECHO, and it helped me acclimate to my new environment.

After checking into my dorm, my first official visit was with the financial aid office in Jesse Hall, Mizzou's main administrative building. An imposing, red-brick building, I could see its white dome from a distance. I was in good spirits and had really sunk into my thoughts about life as I walked. I felt good about the meeting, and I looked at the signs for directions to the financial aid office on the lower level.

As I entered the basement, I was welcomed by a sight that mirrored a dungeon, a dimly lit space with an institutional feel that could have cast a shadow on what was supposed to be a joyous moment. But I felt nothing but joy as I waited my turn. I looked forward to hearing how much extra money I would receive in scholarships that I could apply to my other expenses.

Certainly, I thought, *I can buy a car with the money left over after paying for the dorm, classes, books, and other expenses like gym and health care.* Every Black student I'd known at Mizzou told me they'd received the scholarship, so I thought I was a shoo-in. After all, I was Black, too.

"Orvin Kimbrough," the financial aid person called out. "Yes, that's me," I said enthusiastically, standing up from the wooden bench and moving toward him with a swagger. *Let me go collect my money*, I thought.

After making my way into his office, sitting down, and exchanging niceties while he secured information about me, he delivered the stunning news in what was shaping up to be a dark moment: "Oh, you don't qualify for any scholarships."

"That can't be," I insisted.

"No, Orvin, I'm certain about this. Students who come in on academic probation aren't eligible for scholarships," he said.

I wondered why they didn't tell me that before I got to campus. It would have saved me a trip to Columbia. Now, how would I get back to Saint Louis?

I had worked so hard to get to this point, and my mind was racing. I sunk into a whirlwind of negative thoughts and felt my mood shifting. *The deck is perpetually stacked against me,* I thought. *It's two steps forward, three steps backward.*

"But you do qualify for loans," he said.

I perked up. I'd just heard the word "qualify."

"I qualify for what?" I said.

He said something about a Pell grant and something else about it being backed by the government. He may as well have been speaking a foreign language because I had no idea what he was talking about. However, his tone seemed to indicate that I could stay at Mizzou if I did what he asked of me.

"You need to fill out some paperwork to see how much you qualify for," he said. "Given your circumstance as a ward of the State, you should be eligible for the maximum amount, which will more than cover your tuition, dorm, and other college expenses," he said.

Trembling at the prospect that it would all end there in Jesse Hall, his words gave me a lifeline. I held on thinly to hope that he was correct. *I can't go back home,* I thought.

He gave me the paperwork, something called a Free Application for Federal Student Aid (FASFA), and we worked through the documents together. It was simple because I didn't have any income and no parents. This was my first loan, and I didn't know much about what I was doing, but I felt that by filling out that paperwork, I was making some kind of investment in myself—an investment in my future.

And *bingo!* He was correct. I qualified for the maximum loan amount, so that's what I asked for—the maximum amount. It was like hitting the jackpot. They gave me provisional approval, and I went back sometime later to pick up the surplus—the amount that exceeded what I needed for direct educational expenses. I was overjoyed. The fall of 1994 was a defining moment as my college adventure began.

I walked out of the building feeling hopeful and ready to start my college life. I continued to explore the campus further and set out on a journey to find out where my classes were. Jesse Hall was great, and the rest of campus was equally stunning and unlike anything I'd ever experienced. I'd only known Saint Louis City, with its streets on a grid, many run-down houses, and danger around every corner. The campus was like a park, full of grass and trees with beautiful buildings spread out all over it.

I soon learned that there were actually two campuses. The older "red campus," where Jesse Hall was, felt more comfortable to me because the buildings were made of red brick—just like the buildings at home. Those buildings surrounded a central greenspace, Francis Quadrangle, and the famous Columns stood in the center of the quadrangle. They reminded me of those big columns in front of the Annie Malone Children's Home, but they didn't hold up a portico; they were all that was left standing from when the university's academic hall burned to the ground in 1892, almost exactly one century ago. Students were everywhere, playing frisbee and hacky sack and talking and laughing. They all seemed so happy and full of life.

The other campus was the "white campus," where the buildings were made of limestone. Lowry Mall was between the red and white campuses, with its underground McDonald's and the huge Ellis Library. South of the library stood more modern classroom buildings. In the coming years, I would spend a lot of time pacing this part of campus, which was friendly and inviting, working on projects, studying, and memorizing class notes.

It was hard for me to believe that this would be my home for the next four years, but here I was—ready to major in physical therapy because that was a helping profession similar to my occupational therapy internship in high school. *I'm now a real student at the University of Missouri-Columbia,* I thought. Saying the university's full name gave me chills; it felt like I'd accomplished something great. There was so much stature to that name and institution in my home state of Missouri.

As I thought about those big, white columns and walked around campus that day, I reflected on my life up to that point. The boy who had wanted to be Superman, who had the courage to climb up on that dresser—the tallest point in the room—and jump off, had found that courage again after years of abuse and neglect. I didn't know exactly what I wanted yet, but I did know what I did *not* want. I didn't want to stay in the cycle of poverty. I didn't want a life like some of the kids I'd grown up with—kids who joined gangs, got pregnant, and went to jail. I didn't want addiction. I didn't want any part of the life I seemed to be destined to live, and I was doing it—I was unlocking my future, and college was the key.

I'd been focused on survival for so long and felt like I was constantly living on a fault line, just waiting for the next big quake to come. The Annie Malone Children's Home and ECHO had given me just enough space to imagine that my life could be something better. I started overcoming my fear of becoming like my parents and finding faith that my life had value, purpose, and meaning, and maybe—just maybe—it was part of a story bigger than me. Still, that decision to go to college had been one of the scariest, most challenging decisions I'd ever made, and though I didn't realize it then, my college years would push me in ways I couldn't yet imagine.

I didn't want any part of the life I seemed to be destined to live, and I was doing it—I was unlocking my future, and college was the key.

I'D SETTLED INTO MY DORM, registered for my classes, and secured all my books. Now what? The first few months of college were a blur. I generally had classes on Mondays,

Wednesdays, and Fridays. My nemesis, College Algebra, was back, and so was Biology and Biology lab, which I didn't particularly care for. There were so many students everywhere. This was the first time I'd ever sat in an auditorium with nearly four hundred other students to learn a subject. This was mass-produced education at its best. No matter my study habits, which were being developed and honed, I found myself getting increasingly lost, and the worst part was that I didn't know how or to whom to reach out to for help.

One Laotian kid from my high school, Joey, lived in my dorm. We would connect often. He was a smart kid majoring in engineering. Occasionally, he would help me with my college algebra class, but I was beyond being helped; this class swallowed me like a python does its prey. I felt my very airways constricting with the pressure, anxiously fidgeting as if anticipating Shirley's blow from a wrong answer. Each assignment sent me into a panic because it stood between me and successfully maintaining a 2.0 GPA, which was a condition of my academic probation.

I spent a lot of time in the gym that first semester trying to decompress. Another dorm mate, star football player and former ECHO resident, Earnest Blackwell—who was an imposing six feet five inches and always donned a wave cap—and I spent time together discussing life and girls when he wasn't practicing, at games, or hanging with his teammates.

The campus buzzed with activity, students moving between classes, laughter echoing through the hallways. I, however, preferred the quiet corners of the library. The silence there was comforting, a stark contrast to the chaotic energy outside.

Every day, I followed the same routine: wake up, attend classes, mostly study alone in the library, and return to my dorm. Occasionally, Joey, my dorm neighbor, would drop by to say, "What's up Orvin?" and shoot the breeze, or Earnest would invite me for a ride to Walmart or to pick up food. But these interactions were brief, fleeting moments in an otherwise solitary and welcomed existence.

As I occasionally sat near Lowry Mall, my mind often wandered. I watched groups of friends laughing and studying together, a pang of loneliness hitting me. I knew I was isolating myself, but the fear of deeper connections held me back. "It's safer this way," I thought, "No complications, no distractions."

I had one female friend who provided brief escapes from my isolation. We would meet up occasionally, enjoying casual encounters and conversations that never went too deep. She had a long-time boyfriend back in Saint Louis, and I was content with our friends-with-benefits relationship. I didn't want anything serious. It was a perfect arrangement for me as I, more than anything, valued my solitude.

Over Christmas break, she became more distant. I noticed the changes—less frequent calls, shorter conversations. One day she phoned and confided in me that she was pregnant and would not be returning for the next semester. I could hear the pain in her voice and sense the tears on her face. I sat quietly, the weight of her words sinking in, thinking about her and reflecting on my journey to that point, and how I was fortunate that she wasn't calling to tell me I was going to be a father. When she didn't return, I must admit the campus felt even emptier.

Some days, I didn't know how I was going to make it. I, too, was pregnant with the possibility of defeat. I didn't want to birth this idea. I hadn't yet learned about the student support on campus, and I'm not sure that even if I had known about them, I would have felt comfortable using them. I tried hard to develop stronger study skills. I studied a lot, but was I studying the right things?

At Annie Malone Children's Home, I had chafed against the structure that the institution imposed on me, but college demanded a different kind of structure. Annie Malone had guided my day-to-day—when to wake up, brush my teeth, eat, and what to do with my money. However, college presented a different challenge. College said, "Here's the goal—now figure out how to get there." This, I learned, is so important to achieving anything in life. But first, I had to make it through College Algebra.

My experience with the summer class made me anticipate its difficulty; repeatedly retaking a test-out exam wasn't an option. Now, I encountered numerical expressions, theories, and abstract ideas floating in the air, detached from reality. To add to the challenge, the class was massive, with hundreds of young adults crammed into an auditorium, grappling with the content in what they termed a "weed-out course." *What does that mean?* I wondered. It soon became clear that this course was designed to sift through the masses and determine who was college material and who wasn't. I feared I'd be deemed unsuitable for college if this course was the judge. The thought of asking questions in front of such a vast audience or admitting I needed extra time was daunting. The challenge was formidable. Despite my best efforts, the fear of academic probation grew stronger on test days, weighing me down with intense anxiety. I had one clear goal: to achieve a 2.0 GPA. This became my daily mantra, "2.0," focusing on it every day. I was diligent about my studies and did the very best I could. As the semester ended and I took my last College Algebra and Biology test, I felt that I was hanging on by a thread. I wouldn't get my final grades right away; they were mailed out over Christmas break. I hitched a ride with Joey back to Saint Louis and awaited the verdict on my grades while staying with Joyce.

Soon enough, I received word of my grades. I earned a C in most classes, a B in a history and social studies course, and a D in College Algebra, which is what I expected. *I did it!* I thought. I was certain my B would offset the D in College

Algebra since the classes were weighted the same, but not so fast. I kept reading and realized that not only did I earn a D in Algebra, but I also earned a D in Biology Lab, which was a two-credit hour course. The two classes combined were enough to sink my GPA to 1.8—and my stomach sank. I was in agony.

Shortly thereafter, I received a letter in the mail with the bad news: "Orvin, you earned a 1.8 GPA, and a condition of your enrollment on academic probation was that you maintain a 2.0 GPA. You are being officially withdrawn from the school."

"No! This cannot happen. I'm being dismissed from school," I cried.

I was crushed. I immediately thought about all the people who had cheered me on—the teachers, the state workers, the folks at ECHO who celebrated me "because I was so rare." I thought about my mentors, the people from the church, community-based organizations, my godmother, and others to whom I had proudly declared that I was going to college. They were genuinely happy for me.

So many had invested in me and helped me get on a path to stop feeling like just another poor kid who needed to be stabilized to get through high school, only to be dumped out on the streets of North Saint Louis. "Orvin, you have real potential," they'd often said. I meditated on this statement now more than I had when I was in good standing and in college.

I reflected on the negative thoughts that had been constant during my past sprint to get into college. These thoughts had become characters in my story, convinced that the challenges were too much for me to overcome, at least in the way I wanted. They would remind me, *Your mom was an addict, your dad was absent, you don't have a chance.* Now, I was on the verge of failing the people who championed me and giving life to the negative thoughts that always operated in the background. I was on the verge of living into what the statistics said would become of me. Through tears, I vowed to keep the news to myself, and I slipped into a depression. After several days, I built up the courage to call the Dean of Students. I was so ashamed that I literally begged him to take me back, to give me another chance.

"If you don't give me another shot, I'm not going to make it," I said.

And I meant exactly that—not that I would have to settle into a lower level of success, but that I literally *would not make it*—I wouldn't survive. I felt this deeply. This was a life-or-death moment.

He said, "Make your way to Columbia so we can discuss this."

After hearing my plea that I had no transportation to Columbia and several moments of me throwing myself humbly at his feet, I firmly stated, "I will not let you down."

After hearing me out, he finally said, "OK, one more chance, but this is it. If you can't turn it around in the spring, I don't know what to tell you."

I never spoke about this with anyone. I got through Christmas break, trying to recenter and make myself and those who invested in me proud. Not knowing about my near miss, people were still investing in me, and I learned through ECHO that I would receive a non-interest loan from the Scholarship Foundation to help with my education. It was still a loan, but without interest. This felt great, but the only thing I was focused on as I made the trek back to Columbia was my new lease on life, which had a final expiration date—the end of the second semester. By missing the 2.0 grade point average mark, it became clearer that the world was literally black and white. There was no gray. However, there were people in the world, like this dean of students, who had the power to see gray if they believed the risk was worth it. I was on the borderline of success, and I needed something that was small to others but was big to me. I needed just one more chance. I needed a small gesture to break in my favor.

My 1.8 GPA didn't mean I hadn't tried hard; it meant I fell a little short of the goal. I had never been prepared for college and needed one more shot. I needed one more attempt. One person had the power to do that.

I was on the borderline of success, and I needed something that was small to others but was big to me. I needed just one more chance. I needed a small gesture to break in my favor.

"I will not let you down." I've used those words many times since then and lived into them. When I say it, I mean it. I needed him to believe my words, and he did. I was no longer entertaining the idea that I could fail. To fail was to lose everything I aspired to in life. I knew that this time, I needed to channel my energy differently. By falling just a little short the first time around, I could see success.

I knew I needed greater focus. I needed mental clarity. I needed to align myself with the right people who had the right mindset to win. I needed to see that the numbers affixed to my new address were a real chance at writing a new story.

WHAT I'VE SEEN

All I know is what I've seen
and what I've seen ain't good
am I supposed to be poor
in trouble with the law
and confined to my neighborhood

should I do unto others
as they have done unto me
thus exploit this world
as I've been exploited
and lash out visciously

what have I to live for
if all I see are these streets
when my chances for survival
are limited by
the negativity my hood breeds

is it my neighborhood really
that perpetuates this decline
or is it exactly what I'm forced
to believe if I never elevate my mind

am I truly stifled
by my inadequacies
of monetary means
all I know is what I've seen
until I begin to dream.

CHAPTER 7

"I really don't think life is about the I-could-have-beens.
Life is only about the I-tried-to-do.
I don't mind the failure, but I can't imagine that
I'd forgive myself if I didn't try."

—*Nikki Giovanni*

I was so close to "making it," which meant doing something different to overcome poverty. For me, that something different was college. My oldest brother had gone to college on a football scholarship. Though we never discussed his academic progress, I later learned he didn't graduate until many years later as an adult. I was proud when he finally completed his degree.

When I told the dean of students that "I'm not going to make it" if he didn't let me back in, the truth was that I couldn't picture my life without having a college degree. I needed a college degree like I needed oxygen or water; it was tied to my survival. Perhaps my passion for getting that degree was fueled by the fact that, outside the temporary material success of drug dealers, the most successful Black people I'd seen were entertainers or sports figures. There's nothing wrong with this line of work and the success that comes from it because these people leaned into their God-given gifts. However, I was neither athletic nor an entertainer.

Many successful Black people I knew were gifted tradesmen who made good money. Though I'd been exposed to trades in high school and worked for Mr. Weeden, the first Black business owner I knew who owned a construction company, I wasn't particularly handy. Trade school wouldn't have suited me. My gift was my mind. I'd always been a reflective and serious thinker. I believed I had what it took to be an above-average scholar and leverage that into a meaningful career to transcend poverty.

College introduced me to an eclectic mix of ideas and a diversity of people from varied backgrounds and perspectives. My upbringing instilled in me a propensity to seek out the good in others and connect with those often sidelined. This ability to empathize with people of divergent worldviews paved the way for robust debates, including those around poverty and societal attitudes toward it.

The 1990s often portrayed poverty through a racial prism. Our explorations in sociology and Black studies that questioned whether poverty was a consequence of personal shortcomings or systemic obstacles proved to be eye-opening. These discussions debunked the myth of rugged individualism and highlighted the profound influence of government policies and laws on personal trajectories.

"Is poverty a consequence of one's own doing?" my professor would ask forcefully. We all diverted our eyes, looked down, and tried to avoid being called upon. It was always interesting to see who would speak first.

He repeated the question but added more; he personalized it.

"Is their poverty a consequence of their own doing, a condition of their choices, their lack of intellect, and their lack of effort?"

Looking out at the silent, awkward faces, he said, "Of course not, but some people believe that, and it is a dangerous narrative. Why would we believe this?" he asked.

By this time, I knew he would answer his own question. However, just then, I saw a hand shoot up out of the corner of my eye. It was a young White kid with a stocky build and blond hair.

"Yes, sir," the professor said, beckoning him to speak.

"My great-grandfather came to this country, fought in the war, took advantage of the GI bill, went to school, and started a business." He paused, fidgeting and trying to find his words. "I guess there's a perception that there are people who've been here a long time, and we are taking care of them with our tax dollars."

I'd heard some version of this before. It was the idea that Black people have been provided every opportunity to succeed, but they're still behind because they don't work hard.

My thoughts were sharpening at this point. I'd been exposed to anthropology, which looks at the human experience across time and cultures; sociology, which analyzes social structures, relationships, and institutions within specific contexts; and psychology, which looks at the mind and human behavior.

I had to fight back emotion when I said piercingly, "It's been less than thirty years since laws were enacted to allow Black people to be educated fairly. I wish my great-grandfather had the same opportunity with the GI bill."

I would make this statement more than a thousand times in my life. I was learning in real-time that beyond my impoverished circle, the idea that Americans succeeded based on rugged individualism was real and that there was little account for things like the government and laws that either helped you or hurt you. I'd only been exposed to government assistance in the form of welfare. I now began to distinguish between welfare that helped you produce something and welfare that seduced you to do nothing.

I yearned to learn more about my history, so I immersed myself in as many Black history courses as possible to deepen my understanding of the true narrative of Black history. These classes were unique for me because they were the only times I encountered Black professors. My readings were extensive and uncovered the stories of influential figures like Mary McLeod Bethune, whose parents were once enslaved. Despite such daunting beginnings, Bethune emerged as a pivotal figure in education, women's rights, and civil rights, and she founded what is now known as Bethune-Cookman College in 1929.

Benjamin Banneker's story also resonated with me. Born to a formerly enslaved father and a mother who had been an indentured servant, Banneker's self-taught knowledge led him to become a renowned surveyor, astronomer, and almanac author, proving that formal education is not the sole path to success.

I was particularly struck by the revelation that the first African American to win the Nobel Peace Prize was not Dr. Martin Luther King Jr., as I had thought, but Ralph Bunche. I wondered if he was related to my high school basketball coach, Mr. Bunche.

I was intrigued by Madam C.J. Walker, who was raised in poverty by sharecropper parents who were formerly enslaved. She became one of the wealthiest and most influential women of her time. Starting with just $1.25, she founded a successful hair-care line tailored for African American hair, driven by her personal battle against hair loss.

These leaders taught me a crucial lesson about success: when you start from a disadvantaged position, your effort, focus, and mindset must exceed the ordinary in intensity, duration, and quality. Each of these trailblazers exemplified these qualities and embodied what it means to overcome obstacles and pave the way for future generations.

My world began to change in college. The harder I tried, the more support I garnered, so consistency of effort became my rally cry. Each time I could take extra credit coursework to round out my grades or provide a buffer, I pursued it with a single-minded focus. Even during debates and intense discussions, I never lost sight of the fact that my gift was about actually seeing other people. Regardless of our disagreements, like the idea that Black people don't work hard enough, as suggested by a classmate, I didn't see that guy as a bad person; I simply thought he was misinformed. I leaned into my gift of encouragement.

"You got this," I would say as I walked to test day with my peers.

Not only did I attend classes, but I also worked at JCPenney while I was in college. The managers there were all fairly encouraging. Other than my time at Schnucks, it was the first time I felt a sense of community in a large company.

"You could be a manager at Penney's after college," they said.

Wow, "after college" was a nice statement. Early in my college experience, people helped transform what they saw as my gifts into a market opportunity. Many people in my life took me seriously, even when others discounted me. These individuals went beyond belief and kind words to offer me help. A helping hand, like the one extended by the dean of students or Djaun Robinson, one of my childhood house parents, is paramount to success. Back then, I thought about young people from my neighborhood. So many of us needed the serendipity of meeting one person who took a vested interest in helping us see the possibilities. This entire picture of hard work, effort, and persistence is often futile unless there's also a helping hand. It is, in fact, crucial.

Being inspired to do something versus having the internal drive or motivation to do something are different. Inspiration and motivation have been key to my achievements. I believe inspiration is a potent energy to act that comes from external sources. For instance, my oldest brother was a football player. It wasn't so much the football but his discipline that inspired me. He got up every day and put in the work.

Inspiration is a function of your lived experience. Growing up in North Saint Louis with gangs, drugs, fatherless households, and

This entire picture of hard work, effort, and persistence is often futile unless there's also a helping hand. It is, in fact, crucial.

women who carried a heavy burden but kept moving through all the pain inspires me. Seeing the way the church stepped up to provide food, clothing, and spiritual covering inspires me. The church was the last pillar of hope in our community, which was checkered with payday loans and liquor stores.

Motivation, however, is derived internally; it's the thing that gives you the will to move. Motivation and inspiration are opposite sides of the same coin. I was motivated to get back into school for several reasons, including the fear of the "tried but failed" sign the world wrote on the tombstone of my effort up to that point. Instead, I chose to believe that I fell a little short, not that I was a failure. I saw other people who just barely made it, meaning their grades looked like mine, except for one good break. I was motivated to do what they did and more.

Motivation is a fusion of your foundational upbringing, your environment, and your sense of justice and fairness that compels you to lean in and make steady and deliberate progress against a world that keeps score and can be unforgiving and deadly.

Inspiration and motivation feed off each other to keep you constantly leaning into life—if you allow the momentum to work in and through you. I've seen people who were inspired to act because they'd experienced life's challenges, which were internalized, codified, and projected as purpose.

Years ago, I had the privilege of hearing the CEO of one of the largest companies in Saint Louis speak passionately about his challenged upbringing, which compelled him to focus his energy on improving education. He and his wife have established scholarships at multiple schools. One of my mentors, the person who has meant the most to my material success, once shared that he no longer works for his family or his own benefit. He mentioned that 100 percent of his earnings, which is a fortune, is dedicated to his family foundation that provides targeted investments into helping people and society be better.

"I could invest this money like smooth peanut butter and feel good about making broad investments, or I could invest like chunky peanut butter and feel good in making a real and meaningful difference in the lives of a few," he said. "One is like boiling the ocean, and one is like boiling a pot."

When I was living on the economic margins, working to earn enough money to meet my basic needs was a huge motivator. Aside from my desire to serve people and my community through my chosen helping occupation, I had no idea that work could mean so much more than "money to meet basic needs." What else could there be? I've since learned that, regardless of occupation, once you achieve a certain level of "enough," once you move beyond survival and reach a state of thriving, most people experience a mental and spiritual shift. We're inspired to make our unique mark on the world, to have more control over our lives and time, and to operate more purposefully and passionately, like many of my mentors today.

During Christmas Break in 1994, I turned twenty years old. I was incredibly thankful to have been granted the perfect gift—one more chance by the dean of students. I couldn't wait to get back to Mizzou for the spring semester after the near disaster of my first semester. This was my last shot, and I was emboldened to take on college as a system that was not necessarily for me. Although it was clear I didn't perform well, it was also becoming clearer through the tensions on campus that the university had not appropriately prepared itself generally for Black students and, more specifically, for poorer students who grew up in the kind of educational and economic vacuum I did.

In the period between high school and gaining access to Mizzou, I learned some things about how I learned. I'd learned some things about how to set myself up for success. Now, I needed to convert what I had learned into actionable steps and self-advocacy. I thought a lot about public education and how it did or didn't serve me well in the years leading up to Mizzou and during my first semester at the university. I started to think about life, including university life, as one big chess game. My thoughts about most things were transitioning. I knew the system was set up for me—and anyone who grew up like me—to fail, but even in that, just by the chance that I was born in America, I had it better than most people in the world. Public education, success, and failure were all I could think about during that Christmas break. I recall thinking that public education was produced the same way that cars were manufactured.

"Education is, by and large, mass-produced; it's an assembly line," I'd argue passionately during late-night philosophical discussions.

I thought we lacked the resources to help people like me determine our learning styles and customize a learning experience best suited to our success. I spent most of my childhood and initial college experiences thinking I was a failure and less intelligent than others. It turns out I just didn't have a solid foundation, and as a consequence, I needed different tools, scaffolding, and support. To achieve this, I needed to talk to myself differently, organize myself differently, and channel my energy differently. With the right support, I could lean into my learning style and find success.

I spent most of my childhood and initial college experiences thinking I was a failure and less intelligent than others. It turns out I just didn't have a solid foundation . . .

As soon as I read, "Orvin, you have been dismissed from school," and gathered my composure, I knew what to tell myself. I'd had a lifetime of talking things into being, saying things over and over until they became real. So that entire break, I daily said, *All right. I'm going back; I can do this. I'm an exceptional learner. I just learn differently, and I'm going to figure this out.*

Since this was a game of strategy, I first had to figure out the rules. I'd been so excited to get into college that I never truly understood the rules of engagement. I took fifteen credit hours that first semester because I thought that was expected of me. I knew that with College Algebra looming, I'd need to find more time to study. This course would require my undivided attention. *How can I give this three-credit hour course my undivided attention if I take five courses?* I couldn't. So, before I went back to campus, I phoned my advisor to strategize.

"Do I have to take fifteen credit hours to stay in school?" I asked.

"Oh no," she said. "Twelve credit hours is all that's required for you to maintain full-time status and keep your government-backed loans."

So, I cut back to the bare minimum of twelve hours and then complemented College Algebra with other elective courses that I enjoyed, like history and social work. *The blessing,* I thought, as I signed up for the algebra class, *is this time, I can take the course in a smaller class setting.* This was a huge win. I also enrolled in math tutoring that would take place every day after the lecture.

When I returned to campus in January, I chose an introductory social work class and met Dr. Janice Chadda, whose engagement and interest in my journey changed my major—and my life. I was disconnected in many ways from people and the world around me. Most people, I believed, had low expectations about my potential, given the challenges of my youth and the news coverage of the day. The news often disproportionately highlighted crime and violence in urban areas, which contributed to the stereotype of Black boys as perpetrators or victims of crime. It sometimes perpetuated negative stereotypes and reinforced biased perceptions. Black boys were often associated with drug-related activities in the news, which contributed to the stereotype of Black males as criminals and delinquents.

During this period of increased social consciousness, I often shared with younger poor kids—my siblings included—that to most of America and the world, Black kids were expendable. That meant *we* were expendable. If you turned on the news and watched how people like me were portrayed by politicians and others in power, you'd learn that we had no worth or work ethic; we had no value for life and no values in life. We weren't worth the welfare that only some received, but all were thought to receive.

As I entered my second semester, I was ambivalent about family and my place in the world, yet determined to put forth my best effort to change the narrative of my life. I was proud that I'd made it back, and I became obsessed with how much time I had to live to do what God had purposed in my heart. Both fear and faith motivated me. The fear that was powerfully motivating was the death of Shirley and my mom. I didn't think I had time on my side. Shirley had recently passed, and my mother had died at age twenty-eight. I suspected that would be my fate.

I was inwardly focused and became even more emotionally intense. Though the challenges were formidable, several things served me well. I was exposed to good people after having been isolated the first semester. I adopted a "strengths perspective" about my life and community and channeled my energy productively. A strengths perspective emphasized my capacities, talents, competencies, possibilities, visions, and hopes. Contrast that with focusing on my weaknesses and blaming myself for all aspects of my condition. While I may have been disconnected from people, I was not detached from the outcome I wanted for my life. This mental shift is what Dr. Chaddha, my Introductory Social Work professor, taught me.

One day, I had an epiphany that was reinforced by the memories of my childhood: I had to bottle up the intense emotions that were associated with trauma, failure, and society's neglect and, instead, project an *alternative vision* for my future. I couldn't place my dependence on other people anymore. I needed to draw energy in a different way and become even more of a champion for myself, channeling energy toward activities that would facilitate my advancement. If I focused externally on the environment for inspiration, it was a defiant act that reinforced the world's disdain for my existence. This is what gave me energy. I found that I could not only draw energy from the negatives in the world but also from the positive people I encountered. This was my strength's perspective coming full circle. I leaned into that and the strength of how I learned.

Understanding how you learn, excel, and achieve is an important first step to success. Once you're clear about this, you must relentlessly cultivate these conditions. For many years, I wasn't interested in school, and it wasn't until college that I realized I learned when content was presented in a compelling and practical fashion.

During my college volunteer work at the local Boys and Girls Club, I shared an important message with the young people: "Failing in school doesn't mean you are a failure." I emphasized this point repeatedly and explained that we sometimes struggle because of the way information is presented. However, I always stressed the importance of putting in effort and giving your best. We may encounter subjects we're not passionate about, like College Algebra for me, but overcoming these challenges is necessary to achieve our goals.

Those days were enlightening. I realized for the first time that I loved to learn and was naturally curious. In fact, I could wake up before dawn and study all day by myself without flinching or missing human interaction. I also enjoyed studying in group settings to gauge my learning progress against others. The challenge of their knowledge acquisition spurred me on. I aimed to "outlearn" them and be the one to "set the curve" until years later when I found myself competing solely against my own previous achievements. My learning style required that what I was learning be directly applicable to life rather than being abstract. Eventually, I discovered that I thrive in smaller groups and require a personalized learning plan and framework. Given this, I realized the need to create a structure and system that was repeatable and universally applicable to everything I studied.

And I did.

For every class, I talked to myself, often pacing on campus. *What's the big idea here? OK, how do I break this idea and this content into smaller concepts?* Now that I had the smaller concepts,

I thought about the component parts and the relationship between them. It didn't matter what it was, whether it was the relationship of one sentence to one paragraph or one paragraph to an entire page. It didn't matter if the subject was history or math. I established a structure and a cadence I could remember, then would layer more content and learning on it. This strategy helped me memorize and ultimately learn what I needed to learn.

The semester ended, and I was confident that I'd achieved the outcome that I set out to achieve. I passed College Algebra and did well in all my courses. In May of 1995, I was once again headed home, this time for summer break.

I hopped on the flywheel of achievement that summer and never got off. Staying on that flywheel required consistency and disciplined action. I aligned my actions to create momentum, and as my efforts in the right direction accumulated, the compounding effects over time created a self-reinforcing cycle of achievement.

After my first semester, I learned that I might fall short, but I couldn't frame that as a long-term failure. I needed to frame any failures as what they were—short-term glitches. I simply fell short of victory, and if I continued to project a powerfully compelling vision and was both patient and persistent in my effort, I would ultimately win.

On the car ride home this time, I didn't think about the possibility of failure. Much like the resolve I'd developed after coming so close at the end of the first semester, I resolved to receive all that God had positioned me to take.

That summer, I reflected on the semester and realized what a huge achievement it had been. I thought about the path I didn't take. The easiest route would have been to do what almost everyone else, given the same set of circumstances, would do. *We're likely to take the same path,* I thought, *because it doesn't create visible conflict. This is why so many of my childhood friends ended up selling drugs, why so many ended up pregnant, and why so many ended up dead or in jail or in jobs with no purpose.* Keeping up with the Joneses was alive and well, and it could be a race to the bottom if that's the environment you were born in and are most comfortable with. Even if the common path conflicts with your internal compass, it's the path of least resistance and what you're most likely to do.

If this is the direction for most people, it's easy to see why we can be seduced into thinking this is the right path because this is the norm. Environment is so powerful—even if the common path conflicts with your internal compass, conformity is the path of least resistance and what you're most likely to do.

Inspiration, while crucial, often falls short of propelling us toward making different choices. Witnessing someone from a similar background or facing similar challenges achieve something extraordinary can ignite a spark of inspiration. However, as powerful as it may be, this initial spark is not always enough. I've observed many who are momentarily inspired, only to find themselves back in their comfort zones as the inspiration wanes. For inspiration to translate into action, it requires an engine, a source of continuous energy. I refer to this as an activator. In my experience, the most potent activator that bridges the gap between inspiration and motivation—the intrinsic drive to act—is faith.

Setbacks are a part of the journey, but accepting failure is not. Merely attempting and failing implies a cessation of effort, whereas my commitment is to a relentless pursuit until success is achieved. This tenacity, this unyielding effort, is what I chose to embody. I began to view myself through a divine lens—as

> *Keeping up with the Joneses was alive and well, and it could be a race to the bottom if that's the environment you were born in and are most comfortable with.*

"more than a conqueror." This self-perception, fortified by my faith and reliance on divine love and grace, made me confident in the eventual victory over any of life's hurdles.

Armed with this mindset, I persevered in my academic journey, determined to overcome any obstacles that lay in my path to success and achieving my degree. This journey was not just about education; it was a testament to the power of faith as the ultimate activator, turning inspiration into tangible achievements.

I fully embraced the mantra, "If at first you don't succeed, try, try again," and committed wholeheartedly to its message of persistence and resilience.

WHY'D I MAKE IT

I wonder why I made it and others didn't
Why I persist and others quit
Why when the terrain seems quite the same
I walk forward
Others go backward
And pass the blame
Why when opportunity is abound
And your intelligence is truly profound
And I am average and somehow bound
For adventures beyond my sight and sound
Why at a standstill you are found
Searching for the easy route
Why I often ask myself
Are you focused on immediate self
No thought given to intellectual wealth
And spiritual growth to stave physical death
Why, why, why decry
When you don't even try like I

CHAPTER 8

"If you wanna fly, you got to give up the shit that weighs you down."
—*Toni Morrison*

That summer, I lived with Joyce and worked two jobs. One was with the Division of Family Services, where I worked for Mrs. Marie Thomas, a veteran leader of the Independent Living Program, in which I'd been a participant during my days in a group home. My other job was at Popeye's Chicken. Each day, I relied on public transportation to get to work and either headed to downtown Saint Louis or to North County, a suburb near where I lived.

I had a personal mission that summer. The first part was to save enough money to pay off a maxed-out credit card that I'd foolishly applied for in exchange for a T-shirt. Those credit card pushers on campus didn't care that I didn't have a job at that time or a means to repay; they simply handed me a credit card, and like any teenager, I considered it free money. Consequently, I maxed out the $500 limit and tried my best to avoid their calls throughout the semester. While I felt terrible about it, I was trapped, and my goal was to free myself from that trap. In addition to paying off the credit card, my other goal was to move off campus. To do that, I had to purchase a car to get back and forth to my classes.

At Popeye's Chicken, my wages barely exceeded the minimum rate of $4.25 per hour, reaching only around $5 or $6 in 1995. On the other hand, the Independent Living Program job paid between $10 and $15 per hour, though the hours were limited. I don't know how, but after I discussed my work situation and my ambitious goals for the summer with Mrs. Thomas—particularly the mess I found myself in after each greasy shift at Popeye's Chicken—she managed to work things out and more than doubled my hours. Now, I was working nearly full-time. Fortunately, I genuinely appreciated and valued the work, and the fact that I was earning more money for less time made it all the more fulfilling.

Mrs. Thomas was undoubtedly one of the kindest individuals I've ever encountered. Not only was she an employer, but she also became my encourager and exhorter, and she even facilitated my first-ever paid speaking opportunity. Through this experience, I started to realize the true power of words and writing, that it could be something beyond a mere hobby or form of therapy.

One day, as we were tidying up around the office, Mrs. Thomas, her back turned to me, casually dropped a question that would pivot the direction of my life. "Would you like to keynote at the annual State of Missouri Child Welfare Conference?"

Unsure if she was addressing me, given her nonchalant tone and the fact that she wasn't facing me, I asked, "You talking to me?"

Her response was tinged with a warmth and familiarity that one might find in a conversation between a mother and her child. "Yes, of course, I'm talking to you. Who else would I be talking to? It's just you and me here."

Encouraged by her confidence in me, I agreed but was curious about the details. "Sure, why not? What do you want me to talk about?" I inquired.

"Your life," she simply said.

The task seemed straightforward enough, yet the reality of what I was agreeing to hadn't fully hit me. The conversation took a turn I hadn't anticipated when I ventured to ask, somewhat timidly, "Does this pay?"

"Of course," she replied with a matter-of-fact tone. "We compensate numerous individuals who deliver programs to the State. How much would you charge to serve as our keynote speaker?"

I was momentarily caught off guard, not by the confirmation that there would be payment, but by the notion of attaching a monetary value to my speech that I would get to determine. The idea of being paid for sharing an hour of my thoughts and experiences was both exhilarating and slightly surreal.

I remember expressing my astonishment to Mrs. Thomas, seeking confirmation, "You mean you're *really* going to pay me?"

She reaffirmed, this time prompting me for specifics, "Yes, and what's your fee?"

A fee, I pondered, still processing the unexpected turn of events. When I realized that I was about to be paid around $5,000 for my words, I had a new understanding of the value of my experiences and the power of sharing them. I even invited a young lady, a Golden Girl from Mizzou whom I was trying to impress, to see me speak in front of a packed house at a hotel in Saint Louis.

SPEAKING IN FRONT OF THIS CROWD ushered in a new era for me and was one of the most exhilarating and frightening experiences I'd ever had. I started strong, having memorized the entire speech, but then stumbled midway because I was distracted when someone entered the room.

I paused, regained my composure, and fought through the nerves and shakiness to deliver my message. I don't know if anyone heard what I said, but I felt like I connected with the audience in a way that can only occur when you are your most authentic self. After a standing ovation, I took my seat and reflected on my experience of doing it scared. Yes, I'd been scared, but I'd done it and felt triumphant. Nevertheless, I couldn't avoid my moments of doubt, discreetly reviewing my hard copy under the table, careful not to detract from the ongoing program.

Mrs. Thomas was renowned for her kind encouragement, and from her, I learned two invaluable lessons that day. At the conclusion of the program, her face lit up with a broad smile as she complimented, "You were excellent."

I responded uncertainly, "I don't know," chastising myself internally for the distractions that made me miss key parts of my speech.

However, Mrs. Thomas, with her unyielding support, looked me directly in the eyes and affirmed, "Orvin, you did great." Her simple acknowledgment and the subsequent presentation of my check instantly lifted my spirits.

"You asked for what you wanted, told your story, and received a standing ovation," she said, beaming with pride.

Now I understood the profound importance of recognizing one's worth, even amidst brokenness. I'd never known that there was value in my trauma.

Remaining at the event well after its conclusion, I was approached by numerous attendees who wanted to shake my hand, their gestures genuine and personal. In a heartfelt embrace, one individual whispered, "God loves you." Another expressed admiration, stating, "You are a shining example of what we strive for in our work." Perhaps the most touching interaction was with an elderly lady who reminded me, "We often see ourselves solely as broken, but even in our brokenness, we are human and whole." She shared that she needed her foster children to hear my story and highlighted the impact it could have. In response, I shared my journey in writing as a form of therapy and encouraged her to support her foster children in finding their own unique modes of expression through writing or drawing.

That moment taught me the intrinsic value of pain and triumph and the lessons we draw from them. Our stories have the power to help others navigate their experiences and understand their place in the world. And sometimes, as was my experience that night, sharing these stories can also have the unexpected benefit of financial reward.

Our stories have the power to help others navigate their experiences and understand their place in the world.

Among the scariest moments in my life was when I told my mother that I'd been sexually abused. Yet, when I stood before a room full of strangers and divulged the details of my abuse and trauma, it was equally daunting. One attendee approached me afterward to commend my vulnerability, which moved me to tears.

She said, "We don't often get to pause and see the work we're doing."

Her observation struck me; she recognized my fear but thanked me for humanizing the experience in such a powerful way. This vulnerability was a life-altering experience and has become a defining aspect of how I engage the world. I learned that people are naturally drawn to authenticity and are eager to offer support. Vulnerability, I've learned, is indeed a superpower.

About one month before the summer ended, I'd saved enough to pay off the credit card, which I did and then promptly shredded it. Yes, you read correctly: I cut it up. I'd also saved enough to make a down payment on a car, so I purchased my first car and signed a lease for my apartment. Other than signing for the debt to fund my education, my next big financial decisions were paying off that credit card, purchasing a car, and signing an apartment lease. I made these decisions by myself, and they were very proud moments. True to form, I paid my rent in advance for the entire semester to guard against any temptation to spend money on things I didn't need.

I looked at so many cars and tried to find something I could afford. Most car dealers didn't care that my work was temporary and would end when school started again. They only cared that I had a job. I had to think about whether I could afford the monthly payments during the school year, and I also had to be confident that I would once again receive the extra money I'd gotten the prior year for my student loans. I pushed myself psychologically to believe that I'd get it again. If all else failed, I would work as many hours as needed to support all my living expenses and debt.

I fell in love when I saw my first car, a sky-blue '87 Buick LeSabre. I put $1,000 down on a car that cost $4,999, and I walked off the lot with the car and an interest rate that was nearing 30 percent. I didn't consult Joyce, who I'd stayed with that summer, or anyone else. I knew I'd be moving off campus into College Park Apartments, and since I needed a vehicle, I worked long hours, saved, and bought it. By the end of my sophomore year, I'd paid off the car, and by the end of my junior year, I traded it in for a 1999 Silver Ford Contour. This time, the interest rate was more reasonable, in the 20 to 25 percent range.

During my sophomore year, I found my groove. I'd settled into College Park Apartments alongside a very diverse cast of characters: Ben, a White boy from rural Mexico, Missouri; Joey, my Laotian high school mate; the Biracial Nate; and me, the Black kid from the hood. We had very interesting conversations about diversity, rural vs. urban living, society, music, food, and, more generally, life. Sometimes, we had fights about cleanliness, noise, and weed smoking, which were followed by disputes about who ate what, video game sessions that lasted all day, and having company at all hours of the night in the common space that interrupted sleep.

This period marked a significant chapter in my life and immersed me in a social microcosm that mirrored the broader American landscape in its diversity of thought, appearance, and actions. Within our group, the paths diverged widely: one suitemate enlisted in the military, another made headlines before being incarcerated for armed robbery, and another embarked on the journey of fatherhood after falling deeply in love. My path, distinct from each of theirs, led me to a period of exploration and belonging on campus.

My search for community led me to learn more about Alpha Phi Alpha, the nation's first historically Black collegiate fraternity. During this time, my quest was for diversity. Apart from my roommates, the circles I moved in were often homogenous, split along racial lines with little crossover. In order to connect with Black students, involvement in Black organizations was essential.

Concurrently, I worked nearly full-time at JCPenney and refined my customer service and sales skills. This job reinforced my understanding that success often lies in the ability to sell—whether it's a product, a service, or an idea. Nonetheless, my ambition was to pursue a career fundamentally rooted in helping others despite recognizing the economic advantages of selling and distribution.

The economic disparities among students at Mizzou were stark, yet they did little to sway my aspirations. My aim was straightforward: to graduate, secure a stable job, and achieve a standard of living that surpassed what my mother had known.

My college journey began in the wake of the Rodney King beating in March 1991. I carried a "me against the world" mindset into an era of heightened racial tensions. This sentiment was further intensified by the enactment of the Violent Crime Control and Law Enforcement Act of 1994, also known as the 1994 Crime Bill or, colloquially on the streets, as "Three Strikes and You're Out." This legislation disproportionately targeted Black boys and men, adding a complex layer to my college experience and shaping my understanding of racial dynamics and justice in America.

My aim was straightforward: to graduate, secure a stable job, and achieve a standard of living that surpassed what my mother had known.

Throughout my undergraduate years, the campus was a battleground for intense debates on the constitutionality of Affirmative Action, questioning the merit of those who benefited from it, and discussions around welfare reform, which many perceived as providing incentives against work, particularly targeting Black women. The OJ Simpson trial added fuel to the fire, deepening the racial divide between Black and White America. This polarization was never more apparent than on October 3, 1995, the day OJ Simpson, the former football star, was acquitted in the murders of his ex-wife, Nicole Brown Simpson, and her friend Ronald Goldman. The trial, which had captivated the nation, concluded with a verdict that split the public. In the lecture hall that day, the palpable divide was evident: a sense of disillusionment etched on the faces of White students contrasted starkly with the relief visible among many Black students, hinting at a broader narrative of systemic injustices despite lingering doubts about Simpson's innocence. All these social issues made their way into college lectures, discussions about current events, and college groups, and they defined the culture of my generation.

I determined that my environment was confrontational; therefore, I had to be confrontational, too. I had to act *on* the world but in a different way than during my childhood. I needed to learn everything I could to make the case that I—and others who looked like me—were worthy to be on campus. We weren't out to siphon from others what we didn't earn. We were competent and competitive and would be a credit to Mizzou and society.

At the same time, I had come to believe that a *system failure* had placed artificial barriers around access, opportunities, and success for Blacks in the first place. In class discussions, when I asserted the existence of systemic oppression, prompting the professor to ask, "What is a system?" my answers always illuminated the complex reality of systemic barriers: the laws and rules, both written and unwritten; societal attitudes; and behaviors that, though often invisible, profoundly influence norms, expectations, and outcomes within society. I passionately argued that it was fundamentally unjust for any group to have to justify their very existence, including their right to be part of the campus community.

The more I delved into these issues, the more my confidence grew in asserting my right to exist within a society that often felt antagonistic. I became increasingly assured in my understanding of the world's inherent unfairness, recognizing that those in power typically see no issue with maintaining the status quo, while those without power bear the onerous task of proving they are not defined by their disadvantages—a challenge that allies and progressives often underestimate.

This personal and community struggle against systemic injustice became a deeply personal understanding, not just an abstract concept tied to the community I came from. Many of my professors encouraged identifying flaws in justice, education, and economic systems and collaborating with allies to reimagine and reshape these systems toward equity. They suggested political engagement as a means to enact broad, systemic change, emphasizing the power of legislation.

A pivotal lesson came from Dr. Weems, one of the few Black professors on campus, who stressed the importance of navigating and finding success within the system as it stands. He warned against the trap of negative thinking, such as learned helplessness—the belief in the futility of effort—and victim mentality, emphasizing, "We are not victims. Have Black people been victimized? Yes, but adopting a victim identity means surrendering your power."

Despite the supportive environment created by professors like Dr. Weems and Dr. Middleton—a Mizzou Law graduate and founder of the Zeta Alpha Chapter of Alpha Phi Alpha—the campus culture often felt hostile. A frequent point of contention was Affirmative Action, with some peers suggesting that the policy was the sole reason for the presence of Black students at Mizzou, overlooking the talent and capability of Black individuals. Even under the assumption that Affirmative Action played a role in admissions, the necessity of maintaining performance standards debunked any notion that presence alone was sufficient

Once given a fair chance, success hinges on individual effort, perseverance, and achievement.

for success. My journey through academic probation, flunking out, and being readmitted stood as a personal testimony to the reality that, once admitted, every student must meet the university's performance criteria. I championed the belief that equitable access to opportunities at a public university should be universal. Once given a fair chance, success hinges on individual effort, perseverance, and achievement.

One of the movies I often refer to about the power of chance, grit, effort, and so much more is the 1993 film *Rudy*. According to Wikipedia, *Rudy* is an American biographical sports film directed by David Anspaugh. It's an account of the life of Daniel "Rudy" Ruettiger, who harbored dreams of playing football at the University of Notre Dame despite significant obstacles. There's a scene in the movie where legacy player Jamie, who's given special consideration on the team because his father was a prominent player at the same college, lashes out at Rudy for putting forth too much effort. This leads to Jamie being scolded by the coach and demoted.

Coach Ara Parseghian asked, "What's your problem, O'Hare? What's your problem?"

Player Jamie O'Hara replied, "Last practice of the season, and this asshole thinks it's the Super Bowl!"

Coach Ara Parseghian responded, "You just summed up your entire sorry career here in one sentence. If you had a tenth of the heart of Ruettiger, you'd have made All-American by now! As it is, you just went from third team to the prep team. Get out of here."

I explained to my Black and White friends that it's the individual's responsibility alone to grasp and grow an opportunity. You could either use it to level up or lie down when things become challenging. Most Blacks on campus, like Rudy, used the educational opportunity to level up and achieve their wildest dreams.

In addition to making the case for Black students' existence on campus, I also thought I should lean in and set the pace in my classes and in my life as best I could. So, I never stopped moving. I worked nearly full-time, went to school full-time, studied nearly full-time, and played far less than others socially. I became intentional about having the right relationships as a resource for my success. I knew I couldn't be an island and be successful in this foreign land called college. So, I connected almost immediately with professors who would become a great support system for me.

This is when I crystallized my forever message that hard work is a necessary but insufficient condition for success. We often hear that showing up is half the battle. In college, and as I have learned in life, you have to not only show up but also think and make a good effort. If you do these things, you'll attract the right people who are willing to help you. Having the right people in your life is an important part of the success equation.

Fresh off my best semester yet, I decided to surprise my sister for her graduation, making her the last among us four siblings to complete high school. My oldest brother had graduated a while ago, and my youngest brother had opted for Job Corps, presumably earning his GED there. Last I checked, he was managing life in a studio apartment and working at a fast-food chain, a path that seemed right for him. Despite this, I often nudged him to ponder what "more" could look like in his life.

Having the right people in your life is an important part of the success equation.

It was May of 1996, and as I was driving from Columbia to Saint Louis, my cell phone rang. Given the high cost of daytime minutes, I usually didn't answer calls in the morning. I glanced at the phone mounted in my LeSabre and debated whether to pick it up. After a moment of contemplation and with the promise of more hours at JCPenney that summer, I thought, *What the hell?* and answered.

The frantic voice on the other end blurted out, "Orvin, your brother has been shot. Hurry, we aren't sure if he will make it. He's at Barnes Hospital."

This brother, Cornelius, was about eighteen months younger than me. Confusion and urgency took hold as I pushed my car beyond its cruising limits, the gravity of the situation setting in with each mile. Guilt washed over me for having left him behind, now possibly claimed by the streets. As I navigated through traffic, my emotions ran high, culminating in a mixture of tears and anger. Upon arriving at the hospital, I was met with a grim scene: my brother, surrounded by machines that seemed to be his lifeline, sparked a torrent of questions and a deep-seated need for answers.

"Will he survive?" I asked. Uncertain responses seemed to echo from all directions.

"He's not breathing independently, and there's a chance he might be paralyzed," they said. The gravity of his condition sank in.

"Who's responsible for this?" I demanded, trying to understand the motive and whether justice was being pursued.

Plagued by a relentless stream of thoughts outside my brother's room, the scant details fueled my desire for retribution. My oldest brother and I, driven by instinct rather than reason, contemplated vengeance.

"We should handle this ourselves," we concluded, our faith in the justice system overshadowed by a primal call for action. The impulse to take control, to retaliate against those who had hurt my brother, was overpowering. Yet, as the day wore on, I recognized this urge for what it truly was: a profound sense of helplessness and despair that pushed me toward a path I had no right to walk.

The drive to retaliate was overwhelming, driven by a mix of hopelessness and a desperate desire for control in a situation that had spiraled far beyond my reach. As the day unfolded, it became painfully clear that Cornelius's lifestyle choices had set him on a precarious path. Discussions with his friends revealed

174

a harrowing tale of violence that was hard to comprehend and left me with more questions than answers.

Cornelius had been targeted and shot seven or eight times by two different gunmen. There was no doubt in my mind: this was an attempt on his life, likely rooted in gang conflict. Overwhelmed by this realization, I needed a moment to breathe and seek support. I found myself stepping outside the hospital to call a friend in Columbia, share the painful news, and seek some semblance of comfort.

Upon my return to the hospital, I met Sharon, a woman unknown to me, who said she was the mother of Cornelius's newborn son, Justin.

"What do you mean a son?" I asked, my voice laced with disbelief at this unforeseen revelation.

As I held Justin in my arms for the first time, the weight of our circumstances truly hit me. Here was a new life intrinsically tied to the cycle of challenges and adversity that seemed to follow our family. This moment, cradling my nephew, marked a poignant realization of the enduring struggles that lay ahead, not just for Cornelius and myself but for this innocent life now caught in the web of our complex reality. That week got heavier and heavier as I learned that my little sister wouldn't be graduating high school. (She would later go on to complete high school and college, and I am so proud of her!).

As Cornelius emerged from his coma, the stark reality of his condition became apparent. He lay there, oblivious to the severity of his situation, while the doctor delivered a prognosis that was nothing short of devastating—he was unlikely to ever move below his neck. This news thrust us into a realm of uncertainty and presented a future filled with formidable challenges.

In those moments, my sense of duty toward Cornelius was overwhelming. Despite our diverging paths, the bond of brotherhood was unbreakable. The introduction of his son,

Justin, added another layer of complexity to the situation and amplified the responsibility I felt. The thought of coordinating the care and planning for his and Justin's future was intimidating, yet I determined to forge a way forward to ensure that Cornelius received the best possible care, even if it meant re-evaluating my life's trajectory.

This challenging period significantly transformed my outlook and life's direction. It reinforced my resolve to complete my education and be accepted into the fraternity and pushed me to eliminate distractions and focus more intently on my studies. The connections and sense of brotherhood I found through the fraternity became a source of strength, which helped me navigate through the trials we faced. My recent academic success had already set me on a high, but now I was driven to reach even greater heights, undeterred by the shadows of my past that sought to pull me back. Amidst it all, I learned to balance the weight of my family responsibilities with the pursuit of my personal and academic goals, a testament to the resilience and determination that adversity had instilled in me.

FORGIVENESS

The pain in my past
fell on fertile ground
it was present at every turn that I made
though I've exorcised those demons
and acknowledged my tears
the trauma I will take to my grave
but here I posit my letter of intent
not to resent those who've
brought me such distress
because my failure to forgive
those who've died
and those who live
makes a mockery of
how much I've been blessed

CHAPTER 9

"Have a vision. Be demanding."

—Colin Powell

Returning to Columbia in the summer of 1996, my mind was a whirlwind of concern and determination. I had pressed the hospital staff for information about Cornelius's immediate future. I understood his paralysis, but I needed to grasp the next steps.

"He needs to learn to breathe on his own," they explained and said that a stint in a rehabilitation facility was imminent.

Reflecting on my initial college aspirations, I remembered that I'd been interested in becoming a physical therapy (PT) major, spurred by my high school health studies. Despite discovering the competitive nature of the PT program and facing academic setbacks that derailed that dream, my interest familiarized me with Rusk Rehabilitation Center, a primary training ground for PT students in Columbia.

"If he can get into that place, it would be great," the hospital staff had remarked.

So that became our goal. Securing a spot for Cornelius at Rusk Rehabilitation Center was not just about ensuring he received top-notch care; it was also logistically practical for me. Its proximity to campus meant I could be actively involved in his recovery and support him through this monumental shift in life. My focus on Cornelius's rehabilitation dovetailed with my return to Columbia and shaped a summer defined by responsibility, learning, and the pursuit of a brighter future for us both.

The path to Cornelius's independence involved several key steps: initially, he had intensive therapy to enable him to breathe on his own, followed by further rehabilitation to strengthen his respiratory system and neck muscles, which was essential for him to navigate a motorized wheelchair. Then, we needed to secure a suitable long-term care facility that could accommodate his needs. The road forward was challenging and stressful, but having a concrete plan gave me a semblance of relief and purpose during an uncertain period marked by adaptation.

THIS PERIOD WASN'T ONLY ABOUT Cornelius's recovery; it also marked a pivotal stage in my personal and professional development. My return to campus coincided with an opportunity to dive into the management internship program at JCPenney, where I was accepted. Nudged by a recommendation by Dan, the men's department manager and a fervent Kansas State alumnus, I considered this new opportunity. Dan, who never missed a chance to engage in some friendly rivalry banter, had seen potential in me and recommended me for the program.

Dan and I often chatted during my shifts. On one occasion in the months leading up to summer, he asked me as he slowly walked to my counter, then leaned on the rack filled with Nike Athleticwear, "So, what's your major again?" His curiosity was genuine despite the ongoing Mizzou-Kansas State jests.

"Social work," I replied. "I'm considering grad school but still feeling my way through the core classes."

Dan saw potential in me beyond academia. "You're a hard worker, got plenty of drive—despite being from Mizzou," he'd tease before turning serious. "Ever thought about a career in retail? You don't need a Master of Social Work; you could get a graduate degree in JCPenney."

By this time, he'd stood upright. He wasn't more than 5 feet, 2 inches tall. "You could really go places here," he said.

His question and comment caught me off guard. While I enjoyed my work at Penney's, I had never considered retail as a career. My passion was helping others, and I couldn't see the connection between corporate or retail work and helping others. Furthermore, the financial rewards held little importance to me beyond earning just enough to make ends meet and do better economically than my parents did. *And what's a graduate degree in JCPenney?* I wondered.

Dan was joking with that comment, but his point was that if I applied myself in this environment, I'd advance in my career. His perspective on the opportunities in retail, especially the financial benefits of climbing the ranks from store to district manager, sparked a new curiosity in me because of how he framed it.

"You know, store managers do quite well for themselves," he pointed out, "and district managers even more so." Knowing my background as a foster kid, he added, "This would also allow you to help others in your family."

I tried to grasp everything he said, and my thoughts raced with the possibilities. I remembered the commitment I'd made to my younger siblings that I would prove we could succeed. Intrigued, I explored the internship program he suggested and learned that it covered an array of business aspects, from merchandising to finance. The idea of a lucrative career in retail began to take root.

"What's the catch?" I finally asked, half-joking.

Dan was upfront about the sacrifices, particularly the long hours during holidays and major sporting events.

"Yes, there are trade-offs," he admitted, "but those are also the times we rake in the most revenue. It's all part of being successful in retail. You have to be open when your customers want to shop."

Months later, as I completed the internship, the lessons I learned and my success opened a new realm of professional opportunities. The decision about my post-graduation path remained open, but the exposure and insights I'd gained that summer had undeniably enriched my perspective and equipped me with valuable skills and experiences that would shape my future choices. This juncture in my life underscored the importance of exploration and adaptability, and I reminded myself that the journey ahead was filled with potential and promise, ready to be seized.

As autumn ushered in changes, my life swirled with unpredictability. My relationship with my family, especially Cornelius, evolved as I navigated these shifting dynamics. Despite Cornelius's struggle with his new reality at Rusk Rehabilitation Center, I leaned on Dr. Weems's advice. I encouraged him to see beyond his physical limitations and not view himself as a victim.

I introduced him to Tyrone Flowers, whose story of resilience and faith was profoundly moving. Tyrone,

> *This juncture in my life underscored the importance of exploration and adaptability, and I reminded myself that the journey ahead was filled with potential and promise, ready to be seized.*

a paraplegic law student and future fraternity brother, exemplified a life of purpose and optimism despite his challenges.

181

Tyrone had also been shot multiple times by a basketball team-mate, but he didn't let that derail him. In addition to graduating as an undergraduate and now enrolled in law school, he married a smart and attractive woman, was deeply rooted in his Christian faith, and was focused on helping others overcome challenges. He was living a full life, and that's what I wanted Cornelius to see.

I hoped Cornelius would be inspired by Tyrone like I was, but none of my words of encouragement or connections with inspiring people moved him; there was no reaching Cornelius. After he had stabilized and could breathe on his own, I received a call that he was checking himself out of the rehab center and moving to some place called Winning Wheels, far away in Illinois. Cornelius's decision to transfer to Winning Wheels marked a significant turn when he chose a path different from the support network we'd hoped to provide. His decision, while difficult to accept, underscored the importance of respecting his autonomy.

Cornelius's decision and other family turmoil kept pulling me in and made me ponder deeply. *Could I truly achieve success if I didn't eliminate the distractions of family life?* I reflected on the airplane safety analogy I often saw in commercials: "Put your mask on first." It struck me—I didn't have my mask on. My stability was fragile, and any support I hoped to receive from Joyce was shattered when my caseworker called to check in on me.

"How are you?" she asked.

"I'm fine," I answered.

"Do you need anything?" she asked.

"No, except for money. I work every day, but it's tough," I said.

"Are you still receiving the $200 monthly maintenance check?" she asked.

"No," I admitted, "I thought it stopped after I entered college."

"No, they didn't stop," she clarified. "Let me verify the address where they're being sent."

Apparently, the checks had been sent to my previous address and were cashed by Joyce without my knowledge.

My stomach sank as I slouched over my bed, trying to stifle my emotions. "Are you sure?" I asked.

"Yes, I am," she affirmed. "I need to report this."

I pleaded with her not to report the missing cashed checks, and she agreed to honor my request. When I confronted Joyce, she showed no remorse for keeping my support checks. She believed it was appropriate payback for allowing me to stay in her home and supporting me during my senior year. This revelation ended our relationship and tested my resolve. However, it didn't diminish my love and gratitude for Joyce and her family for their kindness.

Losing Joyce as a confidant was challenging. I had considered her as family, believing she had chosen me too, only to realize I was mistaken. Joyce was always kind to me, and I cared deeply for her. However, I was wounded, and when I was wounded, I often withdrew; it was the way I coped. In the ensuing years, I only spoke to her on one occasion—to introduce her to the woman who would become my wife.

Despite my deep love for my siblings, the years before and during college had stretched the distance between us, and our family bonds weakened and fragmented. This didn't mean we stopped trying to support each other; rather, our interactions became infrequent and lacked the depth that comes from shared daily experiences. We weren't navigating life's ups and downs together or creating new memories beyond our childhood. In many ways, the prolonged disconnection caused the family we once knew to become strangers. On the rare occasions we did communicate, our conversations often found common ground in revisiting our difficult childhood.

"Do you remember when Shirley did this?" my oldest brother Antwon would often recall, a statement that, when involving Shirley, seldom heralded fond memories.

Yet, these shared experiences of adversity were what continued to link us, albeit tenuously. My contact with my sister dwindled throughout my college years, and the gap between Cornelius and me widened further. Our attempts to maintain a semblance of familial connection were dwindling.

At the same time, I retreated emotionally and accelerated my disconnection from others as a defensive mechanism. Most of my interactions had become purely functional. I engaged with others only when necessary, and trust was an even more elusive commodity. This wasn't a new phenomenon in my life, but it became a more pronounced trait, a dominant characteristic that shaped my approach to relationships and interpersonal connections. Since I was unattached to my family, I thought I could curate a group of friends who would serve as quasi-family. However, this approach hinged on the principle of mutual benefit, and when reciprocity was lacking, I invested no more emotional energy to sustain these connections.

Most of us were raised to think relationships with bloodline family are our most important relationships, but that's not the case.

Most of us were raised to think relationships with bloodline family are our most important relationships, but that's not the case. One of my early projects at the School of Social Work was to interview a guy who was openly gay. I connected with him through a campus group and set up the time to interview him.

We met at an off-campus apartment, and I stood outside his apartment for a while and practiced my questions, pacing back and forth. My heart was racing. It was the first time, to my knowledge, that I'd been in a private space with a gay man.

As I walked into the apartment, his bigger-than-life personality greeted me with a hug. "Welcome, Orvin," he exclaimed, "I'm excited we're going to do this."

When we went into his living room, it seemed very small, and the walls inched closer as if to force us closer together. *What's the deal?* I thought. *Why am I reacting this way?* It wasn't until I thought back to the words of one of my openly gay social work professors, who said in jest within the context of a class discussion, "Every gay man you see is not interested in you," that I chuckled silently and relaxed.

Dominic recounted his coming out experience, which was far from pleasant. His relationship with his parents remained strained, and they scarcely interacted with him anymore, which forced him to carefully choose his circle of support.

"That's what it's like for most of us," he said, his body language shifting as he reflected deeply on his experiences. He bowed his head as though overwhelmed by the emotion of it all. "People, including family, can be incredibly cruel. We are real humans," he said.

Our conversation, both recorded and informal, spanned hours. I told him that I shared his feelings of being marginalized. Like Dominic, I often felt like an outsider, estranged from childhood friends and distant from my biological family. By the time we finished our meeting, my perspectives on inclusion and diversity had broadened significantly, which reshaped my understanding and empathy toward all people.

Dominic's journey and my experiences have deeply affirmed my belief that family is not defined by blood ties alone. True family consists of people who actively choose to bond, support one another, and share values, memories, and experiences. These relationships are built on mutual exchange, support, and genuine connection. While some of these bonds may endure for a lifetime, others may not. Joyce was indeed family, but not for a lifetime. The idea of creating a family out of friendships broadened my perspective about what it means to create and sustain meaningful relationships in life.

The connections I formed in my chosen field of study quickly became a cornerstone of my life, fueling a passion for social work that I hadn't anticipated. The field's rich tapestry of history and potential for tangible impact captivated me. I dove into the study of social work's evolution, which could trace its roots to a post-Civil War America where it was largely the domain of women volunteers. This historical journey mirrored my experiences, notably my encounters with a male case manager back when I lived with Shirley, an anomaly in a field I presumed was dominated by female social workers.

The early twentieth century shed light on the limitations of simple charity and propelled society toward a more nuanced understanding of social issues. The Progressive Era, with its diverse ideologies, became a catalyst for the professionalization of social work. The pioneering work of Jane Addams, a prominent social worker, activist, and Nobel Peace Prize winner in 1931, along with her settlement house in Chicago, stood as a testament to this shift. She embodied a holistic approach to helping the impoverished and set the stage for innovative social experiments. Addams was among the first to underscore the idea that proximity matters in shaping how we think about and assist the poor. Proximity is important for working alongside the poor up close to support them, rather than *working on the poor* at a distance. Proximity is important for how we truly see each other and how we empower communities.

When I discovered that the United Way, a familiar emblem from my time in institutions like ECHO and the Annie Malone Children's Home, had established itself as one of the largest early helping organizations, it filled me with inspiration. Learning about the vast network of United Way chapters across America opened my eyes to the scope of organized charity and its potential impact.

My journey through social work was deeply personal and offered a lens through which I could examine my family's dynamics and our collective history. My classes prompted me to reflect on my upbringing and the challenges my siblings and I faced, including Cornelius's decision to move to Illinois and the growing distance between my other siblings and me. These reflections, coupled with the theoretical tools from my coursework, helped me navigate these personal dilemmas.

I invested a lot of time into statistics, learning many concepts like normal distribution, and I recognized its importance in providing a framework for understanding the probabilities of success and failure within populations. Understanding a normal distribution involves knowing that most results are likely close to the average. A straightforward example is school test scores: the bulk of students score near the average, with fewer achieving very high or very low scores. When applying this concept to the success rates within populations, it suggests that most people will lead satisfactory lives and manage to get by, while a minority will encounter significant challenges or achieve extraordinary success.

For individuals with backgrounds akin to mine, the expectation for success is grim; at that time, fewer than 3 percent of children from the foster care system pursued higher education . . .

Applying statistics in such cases illuminated the systemic barriers many, including myself and those from my community, face. For individuals with backgrounds akin to mine, the expectation for success is grim. At that time, fewer than 3 percent of children from the foster care system graduated college, a stark indicator of existing inequities. This realization prompted me to reflect on my path and the broader societal frameworks that shape our destinies, and I was overwhelmed by the implications.

I found myself questioning everything. I pondered why God had spared me, and I revisited my teenage years when I marched with the Nation of Islam to reclaim my North Saint Louis city neighborhood. I questioned whether the practical application of this faith aligned more closely with my current life stage and its relevance to me as a Black man. The predominantly White depictions of Christ contrasted starkly with how I looked, and I questioned why God rarely seemed to reflect my likeness.

This period was marked by ventures into multicultural relationships, which challenged my established beliefs and led me down new spiritual paths. My experiences in dating brought me in contact with various churches and ignited a spiritual journey that urged me to question the beliefs I'd held since childhood. Conversations with deeply religious people about the wide range of Christian denominations introduced a level of complexity to my spiritual understanding. This journey allowed me to frame Christianity in terms akin to academic majors and minors—with Christianity as the major subject and its diverse denominations, such as Baptist, Disciples of Christ, Methodist, and others, serving as minors. I now had a framework to navigate the diverse landscape of faith more effectively.

As I lay awake at night, I realized that my attraction to the Nation of Islam was because they were the loudest group that offered a counter-narrative to mainstream perceptions. They valued Black attributes that society often deemed negative. Their perspective emphasized self-love as a prerequisite to loving others, and they advocated for self-reliance and the empowerment of the Black community. Their teachings about embracing one's inherent worth and rejecting societal impositions resonated with me and urged me to forge my own path to command respect through self-sufficiency.

During this journey, I had a significant awakening. While sitting in Tyrone's apartment, I wholeheartedly welcomed Christ into my life as a young adult. I had been baptized years earlier in my Catholic church, but this was different. I wasn't making this declaration because I was told it was the acceptable thing to do to be compliant as a kid and honor the adults in my life—this was my decision. My focus was solely on the essential teachings of Christ and the Bible, and I was reborn and liberated from the weight of external expectations. College brought the realization that my faith in Christianity needed to actively engage with and address the realities of the present day.

My faith was my support as I journeyed through a world that often questioned my worth and vacillated between recognizing and disregarding me.

In my search, I encountered a Christian community characterized by its compassion and commitment to activism that challenged societal injustices head-on. The churches that struck a chord with me blended the principles of Black liberation theology with thoughtful intellectualism, which deeply aligned with my fundamental values.

The artwork in my apartment—a portrayal of Christ as a Black man and a depiction of a Black father holding his son—signified the resurgence of my faith. These images were a powerful reminder that I should find Christ within my reflection. My reborn faith anchored me and provided a sense of steadiness through life's unpredictable currents. My faith supported me as I journeyed through a world that often questioned my worth and vacillated between recognizing and disregarding me. My faith has opened avenues for forgiveness, deeper connections, and healing longstanding scars and historical wounds. It stands as a testament to the profound capacity for transformation and healing that comes with a renewed spiritual commitment.

Faith transformed into my guiding light, dispelled my fear, and illuminated a path of forgiveness and optimism. It became more than a source of solace; it informed my professional values, which prioritized compassion and understanding over criticism and disdain. This spiritual odyssey became a crucial element of my journey. It infused my decisions and ambitions with insight and conviction.

My revitalized dedication to Christianity seamlessly blended with my passion for social work laid a powerful groundwork to understand others and fueled my determination to rise above the constraints of my past. This fusion crystallized my belief in unconditional love and kindness. I advocated for treating everyone with dignity and respect, no matter their looks, background, wealth, or accomplishments—principles deeply rooted in my faith. It offered a framework to leverage my journey and academic insights to champion societal transformation.

THE FALL SEMESTER WAS NOT JUST ABOUT ACADEMICS but a time to forge deeper connections with the fraternity that had captured my admiration. Planning a party was a strategic way to strengthen friendships, mixing fun with building meaningful connections. Alpha Phi Alpha, known for its legacy of Black excellence and leadership, represented the ideals I wanted to achieve. Luminaries like the Reverend Dr. Martin Luther King, Jr., Thurgood Marshall, and Duke Ellington—all Alpha Phi Alpha men—weren't just historical icons but symbols of the excellence and impact I yearned to achieve.

During our interview, Dominic stressed that it was important to surround yourself with people who value you for being your authentic self. Despite losing some family and friends, he told me with great enthusiasm, "It's easier to operate in the world when you don't have to pretend to be something you're not."

Pledging the fraternity would test my resolve to maintain my identity. It would test my resolve not to lose myself while seeking to belong to a group. When asked why I wanted to join the fraternity, I said it was about the legacy of those who had worn those letters and what they stood for, as well as the brotherhood I needed.

This chapter of my life was a balancing act between academic pursuits, personal growth, and social commitments. The ethos of Alpha Phi Alpha—particularly its emphasis on scholarship, manly deeds, and love for all mankind—reinforced my commitment to academic excellence and finishing well amid the distractions of college life. My path to fraternity membership was more than a quest for belonging; it was a commitment to uphold the principles of excellence, leadership, and service. With no fallback plan and the weight of my decisions more palpable than ever, I remained steadfast in my academic pursuits, driven by the conviction that my future was mine alone to shape through diligence, perseverance, and a clear vision of who I wanted to become. No matter what pressure came my way, I made a deal with myself to choose my future over anyone and anything.

I was accepted into the process with a directive from Big Brother Hypothermia: "Be on campus at this address, on this day, at this time." I had no clue what awaited me, but I made sure to show up on time, adrenaline coursing through me. I wasn't alone; a handful of others were there too, fueled by their own mix of nerves and excitement, as we learned to greet the big brothers by saying, "It hurts my heart, it chills my soul to see a big brother of the black and gold."

Of the group there, not everyone endured the initial weeks; several dropped out early in the journey. That process taught me that details mattered and that I could push myself even further in terms of my physical, mental, and academic limits. The fraternity emphasized "knowing your history," knowing your brother's history, and showing up for each other. It was also the first time I was exposed to the poem "IF" by Rudyard Kipling: "If you can keep your head when all about you are losing theirs and blaming it on you, if you can trust yourself when all men doubt you . . ." This poem became a powerful anthem for me.

In the spring of 1997, alongside three others—Kevin R. Brewer "Insomnia," Jeremy S. Scott "Deep Freeze," and Marvin Banks "Lord Gibraltar"—I, known as Mr. Biggz, crossed the symbolic burning sands into Alpha Phi Alpha and became an Alpha Man. My initiation marked one of the most profound emotional and mental experiences of my life, and it birthed a bond with these young men that would endure. Through this rite of passage, we crafted a brotherhood to last a lifetime.

Fraternity life exceeded my expectations, offering me instant brotherhood and, to some extent, sisterhood through the connection with the ladies of Alpha Kappa Alpha Sorority, which was founded two years after the "bruhs" on January 15, 1908. However, there was one aspect I hadn't fully appreciated at first: the level of visibility akin to campus athletes that Black Greeks enjoyed. This visibility made social interactions easier, from dating—where I frequently dated different people without much focus on commitment—to securing leadership roles within both the School of Social Work and the fraternity.

I served as the dean for the incoming line and guided new recruits through their initiation process. S.S. Hexakis Stasis, Spring 1998, was the 30th Dynasty and included some exemplary brothers: Keith Terry "Anubis," Brandon Williams "Mr.

Mythodical," Andre Byers "Gold Standard," Brian Lavender "Ice House," Phillip Hickman "The Chapel," and Azubuike Ukabam "Golden Eye."

As a neophyte myself, it was rare and humbling to lead the development of such recruits. I took the responsibility of guiding these brothers seriously and felt deeply honored by the process. I'm still in touch with many of them today, and I'm proud of the remarkable men they have become: lawyers, entrepreneurs, educators, world travelers, businessmen, husbands, fathers, and community leaders.

These experiences taught me a crucial lesson about leadership: you're always under observation, even when you least expect it. It also taught me a lesson about celebrity. While wearing letters across your chest definitely provided an external notch, if you don't feel good about yourself on the inside, letters on the outside can do little to heal that pain. Additionally, it reminded me how easy it was to lose focus when you achieve goals.

While in the fraternity, I chose to pick my moments to plug in deeply and didn't respond well to peer pressure, holding true to my initial commitment. This brought its fair share of criticism. While deeply involved in fraternity life, I managed to maintain an identity independent of it. In addition to my studies, I wrote more, recited poetry at local clubs, and spoke more about my life across the State of Missouri. My first vacation was a spring break trip to South Padre Island in Texas alongside my fraternity brother J-Scott and the two girls we were dating at the time. J-Scott eventually married the girl he brought along. Although my relationship didn't endure, the girl and I managed to maintain a friendly rapport.

As graduation loomed, I found myself at another crossroads and pondered my next steps. The conversation with Dan about starting a professional career at JCPenney resurfaced. After several discussions with JCPenney's Human Resources department, which resulted in a job offer of $30,000, I hesitated and argued that the offer was for less than my student loan debt of $31,000. This reasoning might have been a lapse in judgment because I didn't realize that my student loans weren't due all at once. Nevertheless, the idea of earning less than my debt troubled me. JCPenney eventually increased their offer to $31,000, citing my participation in their summer program as the reason for the increase.

Despite the allure of the offer and the recognition of being wanted, I decided against it and chose, instead, to pursue a Master of Social Work. I believed this path would align more closely with my goal of helping people and my passion. I truly believed that if I pursued what I was passionate about, I would ultimately earn a reasonable and likely higher wage post-graduation. So, I left my retail career for a position more aligned with my aspirations. This led me to work for Integration Plus (Planned Living with University Support), a program supported by the Department of Mental Health for kids with dual diagnoses.

Working my way up to a supervisory role, I encountered young people who were often a danger to themselves and others. One of my first kids frequently muttered, "Kill mom, dad," his speech slurred and difficult to understand at first. Despite his challenges and aggressive tendencies—such as an obsession with tornadoes where he would aggressively spin toys or himself in imitation of being caught in a twister—I found a profound sense of fulfillment in this work. It was tough, but it echoed the complexities of my experiences growing up in environments like the Annie Malone Children's Home.

Unbeknownst to me at the time, my life was about to take a significant turn after attending a pay-per-view Mike Tyson fight at a fraternity brother's duplex. I arrived early to ensure I had a place to sit because everyone wanted to see Iron Mike fight in the mid-1990s. As usual, I was right to plan; the first floor was packed. In addition to the fight, I had a romantic interest in one of the young ladies I knew would attend the event. She was a part of the sorority Delta Sigma Theta, founded in 1913, as one of the original Black Greek letter organizations.

However, as the evening progressed, I noticed a different, brown-skinned woman sitting on the arm of the loveseat just feet away from me, who I would learn was a part of the same sorority. She wore a pleather jacket and nicely fitted pants. Her hair was perfectly styled, and her eyes, a striking shade of hazel, caught my attention. She was petite, around five feet tall, with a fit physique that her attire accentuated, though she wasn't overly curvaceous. Our conversation began somewhat playfully, if not cheekily, as I teased her about her "real hair and real eyes" and made light-hearted jabs about her faux leather jacket—remarks likely inspired by the lyrics of a 1990s rap song that echoed in my mind. She responded to my teasing with good humor, and though the night passed without any significant developments, Tyson's swift victory in the ring was the highlight of the evening.

As the eventful night drew to a close and I made my rounds of goodbyes, I cast one last glance towards "Faux Jacket," half-hoping for a sign that there might be something more between us. Yet, the moment passed without incident. We went our separate ways, leaving the possibility of what might have been hanging in the air. This uneventful ending prompted me to continue navigating the dating scene, eventually becoming semi-exclusive with a different girl who was both enjoyable company and kind-hearted. We shared a lot of time together, and as my graduation approached, the concept of companionship beyond the college experience began to take root in my mind. Despite my previous tendency to keep others at a distance, I became increasingly receptive to building a closer, more enduring relationship.

After firmly deciding to pursue advanced studies, I explored options beyond Mizzou and considered Saint Louis University (SLU) and Washington University in Saint Louis (Wash U). Doubts crept in about my chances of being accepted into either Wash U or SLU, coupled with the realization that I'd already established myself as a known entity at Mizzou. The idea of beginning anew weighed heavily on me as I researched these institutions.

I finished well and concluded my undergraduate journey successfully, yet this milestone, though significant, felt somewhat hollow because it no longer matched the height of my ambitions—to pursue excellence to its fullest extent. On my birthday in December 1998, I reached a goal that had once seemed beyond my grasp—I received my Bachelor of Social Work degree. Because I had reduced my course load to twelve hours, doing so required an additional semester, so the occasion was somewhat anticlimactic, both emotionally and in terms of practical impact. My attention was already fixed on conquering the next challenge, which was to complete the graduate program at Mizzou in only a year and a half to make up for lost time.

I applied to and was accepted into the graduate social work program at Mizzou, fueled by a passion for addressing the broader issues that social work dealt with, like systems change, policy, organizational and people management. I studied macro social work. This field differed from micro social work, which focused more on helping individuals and families navigate the world. I remember when I said that I was going to be a social worker, how excited people were, thinking I would be good at counseling kids. Far from it, I knew early on that I would be no good at direct service. The macro aspect I pursued was centered on management, systems thinking, and what I would later recognize as organizational psychology.

I advanced beyond the average expectations, even among those deemed "prepared"—a stark contrast to my unprepared beginnings at Mizzou. The guidance and wisdom I received at the Annie Malone Children's Home, ECHO, and throughout my educational journey were profound gifts. These experiences, coupled with the critical ability to harness such resources, initiated my healing process from the systemic pressure that burdens those at the lowest end of the preparedness spectrum. Life's uncontrollable aspects, like the circumstances of my birth or the scars from the foster care system, can severely impede progress, resembling Superman's vulnerability to Kryptonite. Yet, reflecting on Superman's lore—where Kryptonite symbolizes the gravity of his lost home—I realized that our past hardships can impact our resilience rather than dictate our destiny.

It had been months since the new calendar year began, and I hadn't given much thought to the encounter with the mystery woman, "Faux Jacket," whom I'd met at the party. However, one day, we reconnected. It was now spring. As I emerged from the School of Social Work building in a secluded part of the campus, I bumped into . . . um . . . *What's her name?*

I realized that our past hardships can impact our resilience rather than dictate our destiny.

I remembered her face and the context of our conversation at the Tyson fight months ago, but I didn't remember her name—bad form.

We struck up a conversation, and I heckled, "Why are you in my building?"

She said she was taking an organizational theory class as an elective, and this just happened to be where it was offered. Finding no other words to keep the conversation going and clearly feeling some level of attraction to this woman, I exuberantly said, "I get a hard-on for organizational theory."

I couldn't believe that I said those words. Yes, those words exactly. This probably goes in the books as one of the worst pickup lines ever!

She froze, looking shocked. "What?"

I took the liberty to explain further and said, "I love social work and the theory that underpins it, particularly how organizational systems impact people." I felt myself emerging from that mental rut, now thinking more clearly. As we were about to part ways, I mustered the courage to ask for her phone number.

She hesitated, questioning, "Orvin, do you even remember my name?"

I winced at the truth and was shocked that she remembered mine. "We both know the answer to that," I replied softly.

Admitting that I didn't recall her name, despite our thirty-minute conversation by the nondescript concrete building, I made a futile effort to recall it before she prompted me, "Do your research."

I jokingly asked her not to hold it against me. Eventually, I gave her my number and asked skeptically, "Are you going to call me?" I repeated the question like an insecure teenager several times as we went our separate ways, focused in her direction as I walked backwards, trying not to trip while making my last plea, "Will you call me?"

She called that night. Actually, her first question was, "What's my name?"

"Latriece is your name," I thundered with the confidence of someone who was connected and could find things out. Before I had even gotten back to my apartment, I had called around to my fraternity brothers and found out that her name was Latriece. One of them later quipped, "She is out of your league." Perhaps, but I felt almost immediately that this was different.

We talked into the wee hours of the morning through stints of silence, which invariably meant one of us had fallen asleep. I learned that she was a business major, accounting to be exact. She was at the end of a five-year program where she would emerge with a master's degree in accountancy. She was an only child, and both her mom and dad were still in her life, though she had a strained and complicated relationship with her dad. I learned that she had a big family and loved her grandma, and since her early teen years, she'd been in a couple of long-term relationships continuously.

During those early weeks, I spent every waking moment with Latriece, and every moment when I wasn't with her, I was thinking about her. Latriece was serious-minded. She wanted something out of life. She was going to succeed because she had a certain discipline about her. This intensified my attraction. This was what I needed in my life: someone who had a sense of purpose and a strong work ethic and who could make it without me because I still believed my life would end prematurely.

One day during those early weeks, we went to Walmart to buy a few items. While standing in the checkout line with our purchases, she unexpectedly added a candy bar.

I jokingly protested, "I'm not paying for that candy."

She replied, "Quit playing."

I reiterated more firmly, "I'm not paying for this candy bar."

What started as a jest quickly spiraled out of control, and I grew frustrated at the swift shift from request to demand. In my mind, I was determined not to be pushed around. I thought to myself, *I'm not a defenseless kid. I need to stand my ground!*

She then suggested, "Fine, give me the keys to the car so I can get my wallet."

I refused.

By now, the checkout cashier's face was flushed, clearly flustered by the charged atmosphere between us. It didn't take long for me to realize my mistake and take responsibility for the situation's escalation. We returned to the car, and she asked me to take her home. That night, we didn't speak. Shortly after, I discovered that she'd reacted to what she perceived as a controlling demeanor. While I was at fault for initiating the conflict, I reacted to what I saw as a demanding attitude. This pattern repeated itself multiple times in our relationship.

We were several weeks into our relationship by the time of the Walmart incident. I had already playfully asked her to marry me repeatedly on multiple occasions, drawn to her strength. However, something about that Walmart incident made me pause. I wasn't certain if we were the right personality fit—two strong-willed individuals who had recently met. In my mind, I pondered, *What are the chances that we can overcome the odds and lead a successful life?*

Despite our differences, we worked through that spat. After the thirteenth time of playfully proposing and her saying yes, I decided I should probably get a ring. I went to Columbia mall, opened a line of credit with Kay Jewler, and bought her a ring. I spent $5,000 on that ring! It was a nice diamond, less than one carat, with a gold band, and it was perfect.

Latriece always wondered why I asked her to marry me so many times and why I didn't have the courage or confidence to make one definitive proposal. There were several reasons, but mostly, being emotionally vulnerable up close was challenging to me. I displayed the symptoms of someone who'd endured a traumatic life. Managing my emotions, memories, and anxiety from years of abuse was a struggle. Negative thoughts were my constant companions, and I worked hard to cope with them. Often dealing with mild depression, feeling numb, disconnected, and unable to trust, I was known to push relationships away before they became too intimate.

Latriece and I represented polar opposites when it came to navigating romantic relationships. She was capable of deep love, whereas I found myself wrestling with it. In a display of youthful naivety, I would often declare at the outset of any relationship, "This won't last," setting a tone of inevitability.

The longest relationship I maintained during my high school and college years spanned nine months give or take, as I habitually shied away from emotional depth to avoid potential pain. Before my union with Latriece, I ended a relationship under less than admirable circumstances. After a brief hiatus meant for reflection, I told the woman I was dating, who happened to be White, that I'd gotten married. This thoughtless act remains a point of regret for me. While I did harbor feelings for her, my actions were driven by a compulsion to guard myself against vulnerability, mirroring her cautious approach to our connection.

I also acknowledged the challenges with family. I didn't have a deep connection with mine and didn't want to struggle trying to form a deep connection with hers. After visiting her hometown, I wasn't under any illusion that it wouldn't be more difficult than usual. Navigating a multicultural relationship felt like handling a sealed box with unknown contents; you can guess what's inside, but you can't be certain until you open it, and the uncertainty itself is intimidating. Open and honest communication was already a challenge, and the complexity of our relationship was not something I felt equipped to deal with on top of all the other typical relationship issues.

I needed to be authentically me, and she needed to be authentically her. So I walked away between breaths. As she inhaled, preparing to reengage the relationship as I later learned, I exhaled and let go.

Four weeks into dating Latriece, my fears seemed to materialize, and they shook the foundation of my trust. I discovered that she had ended a long-term relationship with

her high school sweetheart just a day before we met—a rela-
tionship that had continued on and off throughout college.
The revelation left me heartbroken, and I felt as though I'd
been deceived. If I'd known this from the start, it would have
deterred me from pursuing her seriously, as my insecurities,
fear of abandonment, and reluctance to embrace vulnerability
loomed large.

However, rather than retreating, I came to an uncon-
ventional solution. I decided the logical step was not just to
continue dating but to accelerate things—to move in together
and get married, despite only having known her for a short
period. This plan, oddly enough, seemed perfectly rational
to me at the time and was driven by a yearning for genuine
companionship.

Then, one summer day, on my thirteenth proposal,
Latriece finally acquiesced with a playful, "Boy, I said yes, I
would marry you."

That's when I presented her with the ring and solidified
our commitment. She was taken by surprise that my playful
asks had manifested into a ring. I don't think either of us had
anticipated this gesture of commitment so soon. I didn't know
exactly what I was doing, but I felt like I needed to do it. It was
another one of those "do it scared" moments.

"Of all the girls, why me?" Latriece once asked. We had a
connection I didn't have with anyone else. She was stubborn
when she set her mind to something and appreciated my kind-
ness. Early in our relationship, within about two weeks, I paid
off her $5,000 credit card bill. While I did it because I cared
for her and didn't want her struggling to work to pay the card,
I also paid the bill as a test. She didn't pull away; in fact, she
didn't budge one way or another. She stayed right where she
was—close. She appreciated my spirit and drive, and never
once questioned whether I would do what I said I was going
to do. She showed care and concern for her friends. She didn't

drink much, and she didn't run the streets. She was thoughtful, often cooking or just hanging out with me wherever I wanted to be. She loved God. She was firm in what she wanted out of a relationship. She was introspective about her mother, father, and grandmother. She showed depth in her emotions and thinking. She was attractive. She was the best of every girl I had ever dated and more. She was real; what you saw was what you got, beyond the hazel eyes, of course. She was a perfect 10 for me, and she was definitely out of my league!

I'd met Latriece at a critical time in her career. In addition to finishing up her graduate program, she was taking tests for her Certified Public Accounting (CPA) license, a prerequisite for the long-term viability of her career. During our courtship, she was distracted from school and didn't do as well on her CPA exam as she could have. However, her academic track record was stellar, and she'd landed an audit job with a top-four accounting firm in Saint Louis, locked down an apartment, and scheduled her move-in date.

When I gave her the ring just before her annual family reunion, I insisted that she move in with me, delay the move to Saint Louis, and marry me as soon as possible. I'd never experienced a love like what I felt. I feared losing her if she moved back to Saint Louis without me, and I wasn't willing to take that risk.

Latriece and I got married within three months of our unlikely encounter in front of a nondescript concrete social work building. She was twenty-two, and I was the older man at twenty-four. On a sunny day, June 4, 1999, we both took lunch breaks from our jobs in Jefferson City. At the time, she worked for then-State Auditor, Claire McCaskill, while I was an intern at the Missouri Association of Social Welfare, an organization that advocated for equality and social justice in Missouri. I don't recall much about the ceremony. The judge asked if we were there of our own free will, and we both said yes. We signed some papers, left the courthouse, had lunch, and returned to work. I never mentioned it to anyone on campus. Latriece hadn't yet told her mother, and we didn't want the judgment of people saying, "But you've only known each other for three months. What a challenge!"

We lived in our college town for a few months, and we wrote down the vision we had for our family—a vision that would be so different from our parents'. We doubled down on our commitment to not relent regarding what we wanted to achieve personally and professionally before we moved to Saint Louis for her job. I commuted back and forth to Columbia for a year and worked at Integration Plus to complete my first graduate degree, a Master of Social Work.

Within the first three months of marriage, we finally told her mother. However, we kept our prior nuptials a secret from everyone else, including her curious large family, at the next year's family reunion. Her mom was devastated to have missed this important day in her daughter's life. Latriece was her only child. Our aim had always been to have a proper church ceremony, so we opted for a church wedding one year later at Mount Beulah Missionary Baptist Church in Saint Louis. It was a joyful yet complex time in our young relationship, but it marked a beginning—our beginning.

THANKS

How tremendous it is to extend this thanks to you
for all that you've done
the support you've given both past and present
and the support you've pledged to come
journey with me through a moment in time
and feel as a child what I felt,
disadvantaged,
because I was a product of
abuse and parental neglect
all I needed was an opportunity,
that which you've helped to provide
and with the platform that I now stand on
my potential, I will maximize
you've touched me in a place
that for years I'd hesitate
to let any one near for fear
they would exploit
my vulnerable state
whether your heart lies with the young,
differently abled or the aged
I extend a thank you from us all
for the chance that you gave.

EPILOGUE

"I will instruct you and teach you in the way you should go;
I will counsel you with my eye upon you."

—*Psalm 32:8*

The single most consistent question I'm asked is, "How did you make it?"

I've heard comments like, "You are a one percenter or three percenter—but not in the way people might think." Less than three percent of kids who age out of foster care complete college.

"Considering all the challenges you've faced, you're entitled to not be okay," a person once shared.

"How do you stand in front of people and share those intimate details about your life?" another person asked with concern.

I share my story because it's ultimately not about me. I hope to establish some common ground with people so they will see themselves in me and think, "If Orv did it, I can do it."

As I push past twenty-five years of marriage with the same remarkable woman, I reflect on a journey brimming with ups and downs. The biggest challenges we've faced—the source of disconnection at times—include my demanding work schedule, inadequate communication, and the struggle to keep the torch of our relationship lit. There were moments that nearly drove us apart and mistakes from which we've learned, yet we consistently chose to stay together. Being in a relationship, any relationship, should be an intentional choice, not solely driven by emotion.

Latriece gave me two beautiful children. Having a love like this is akin to the love that our Heavenly Father feels for us. Becoming a father is unlike anything I had ever experienced. When I thought I was out of love to give, it kept growing, expanding beyond what I imagined possible. The love I feel for my children is boundless and continually replenishes itself. It's a profound and transformative feeling that drives me to work as hard as I do. My dedication and efforts are all aimed at ensuring that my children and their children are well-positioned for a successful and fulfilling future. This love is the reason I strive relentlessly, providing them with the opportunities and support they need to thrive.

Blessed with two children now in their early twenties, I am beyond proud as they navigate the complexities of college life, ponder their future careers, and aspire to contribute to the world. Having our daughter was the biggest blessing in my life. As a baby and throughout the years, she has brought immense joy and meaning to our lives. Our daughter, Maddison, an avid reader, has completed her undergraduate studies, graduating cum laude. She now has her ambitions set on law school. Whatever she chooses to do as a profession, my advice to her is to focus and follow her passion. If you are passionate, you will create a mark and earn sufficiently to thrive.

Meanwhile, having our son was God's ultimate gift to me. As a little boy and even now, he loved to push the limits. It didn't matter what the limits were. While I always knew I wanted a son, it was also always the most intimidating task. *How would I help a boy navigate to manhood without having appropriate guides myself?* I wondered. I have tried to be transparent with my son about my shortcomings as a father. I have had difficult conversations with him about what it means to be a responsible man. I have been clear about my expectations of him, for him to learn not just from where I succeeded but also from where I've fallen short.

Our life unfolds in the heart of Saint Louis . . . Embraced by a park-like, green expanse to the east and the vastness of a twenty-plus-acre lake to the south, it's a stark contrast to the humble community where I was raised.

Matthew is in his upper years of business and marketing in college. He started a business during his freshman year and is thriving academically. He is the young man of a million questions. My advice to him is to never stop asking questions and absorbing the wisdom of the elders. Follow your passion, and if you do so, you will leave your mark and earn sufficiently to thrive. Latriece, my partner in this journey, has carved a low-key but significant path in the nonprofit sector, which has enriched her work life.

Our life unfolds in the heart of Saint Louis in a tranquil Spanish-style home spanning over an acre. Embraced by a park-like, green expanse to the east and the vastness of a twenty-plus-acre lake to the south, it starkly contrasts the humble community where I was raised. Nestled within an older neighborhood, our home is a hub of warmth, dreams, and gatherings. These days, Latriece and I weave our time between work and hosting a mix of business clients, family, and friends while seizing every opportunity to discover new people, places, and things through travel.

My choice to pursue a degree in social work was one of the most impactful decisions of my life. The education I received laid a solid foundation for every professional role I've assumed since then. Among the valuable skills it instilled in me, understanding human behavior—what drives people forward or what impedes their progress—stands out as particularly influential. My studies in social work have heightened my sensitivity to the struggles of the vulnerable, the oppressed, and those living in poverty, and they have enabled me to grasp more profoundly the underlying causes of some of society's most persistent challenges. I've learned that financial stability—or the lack thereof—plays a crucial role in determining individual opportunity and is often a root cause of the difficulties many communities face. My background in social work has equipped me for every step of my career journey, enriched my perspective, and enhanced my ability to make a meaningful difference in the lives of others.

Earning my Master of Social Work was not the culmination of my educational or professional journey; it was a pivotal point that led to further academic pursuits. Motivated by a deep interest in differentiating myself and having more options for my work beyond the perceived constraint of a single degree, I expanded my horizons. I earned a Master of Business Administration from the University of Missouri-Saint Louis and a Master of Arts in Theology from the Aquinas Institute of Theology, all while managing the demands of full-time employment. The foundational lessons from my early years in academia—hard work, the importance of continuous learning, resilience to persevere, and the drive to constantly improve—have served as cornerstones for my success in every endeavor. Life, I realized, revolves around systems. Perhaps that's why I once told Latriece that I had a strong interest in organizational theory. Systems intrigued me because I saw that once you master one and learn to operate within it using the cards you've been dealt, it no longer controls you. Unfortunately, not everyone grasps this concept.

I have dedicated my life to helping others understand the full scope of their environments, both positive and negative, and to developing strategies that leverage their strengths to navigate the challenges presented by their circumstances. I believe that no system is an inescapable trap. It contains within it the keys to freedom, all of which are attainable.

Throughout my journey, I have faced numerous challenges—racial discrimination, economic hardship, years of abuse, and trauma. However, I was fortunate enough to find exceptional mentors and counselors who recognized my potential and were willing to support me. An integral part of navigating the system involved connecting with other people who could illuminate the path forward and guide me through the darkness with their wisdom and experience. My experiences with Shirley were also valuable. Recognizing that adversity might always be a part of my life, I consciously decided to strive for success.

This understanding empowered me not only to gain admission to college through persuasive communication but also to excel there, notwithstanding a close call during my initial semester. Intuitively, I recognized that education held the key to my future, and I was unwavering in my determination to seize it. Regrettably, many individuals struggle to discern the rules governing the systems around them and fail to uncover strategies to overcome them. They begin to perceive statistics as certainties rather than probabilities, which is a misconception. Being born into poverty doesn't equate to a lifelong sentence of poverty; it merely heightens the probability of enduring hardship, and the longer a person remains within their existing system without seeking avenues to thrive, the more probable that outcome becomes.

After earning my MSW, I took on a series of intriguing and significant roles. My first major position was with the Vashon/JeffVanderLou Initiative. This project aimed to revitalize a north Saint Louis neighborhood defined by Jefferson Avenue to the east, Vandeventer Avenue to the west, Natural Bridge Avenue to the north, and Martin Luther King Drive to Delmar Boulevard to the south. The initiative sought to infuse new hope into a community that had faced consistent disappointment due to long-term underinvestment. The project's primary goal was to build human capital as the cornerstone for community and economic development. We concentrated on investing in education, health, and skills development to empower individuals, thereby strengthening the economic and social fabric of this community. We believed these investments laid the foundation for a more innovative, productive, and cohesive region, promoting sustainable development and enhancing the standard of living for all community members. This work gave me profound insights into how financial resources impact political dynamics. I also learned that politics alone cannot bring about the necessary transformation within a community.

Following my time with the Vashon/JeffVanderLou Initiative, I transitioned into the role of executive director at Faith Beyond Walls. This visionary project was inspired by Pope John Paul II's visit to Saint Louis in January 1999. It emerged from a collaboration among three local entities: the Interfaith Partnership, the Saint Louis Metropolitan Clergy Coalition, and the Danforth Foundation. The initiative aimed to create a faith-inspired volunteer marketplace that deeply resonated with my values. Faith Beyond Walls sought to connect volunteers from various faith traditions with short-term projects in urban settings that fostered community and service across denominational lines. The project focused on building high-impact relationships among individuals from diverse faith

traditions and economic backgrounds. We believed this collab-
orative effort could help address longstanding racial, religious,
and economic tensions in Saint Louis. Social capital, rooted
in trust, reciprocity, cooperation, and mutual respect, can sig-
nificantly influence economic and social outcomes and can
contribute to the region's quality of life, economic growth, and
overall vitality.

During my time at JeffVanderLou, I worked alongside reli-
gious leaders who equipped me for the immersive experience
I would encounter at Faith Beyond Walls. Once I received the
green light from the Danforth Foundation's staff, who financed
the organization, and from Marylen Stansbery, the initiative's
inaugural part-time director, I had the chance to engage with
Reverend Jack Danforth. As an individual with a diverse back-
ground—being an Episcopal priest, lawyer, author, and former
US Senator from 1976 to 1995—Senator Danforth offered a
rich and varied insight into our conversations.

I met with him in his office in a notable downtown Saint
Louis building, a place I had visited several times before with
Yvonne. She was a former community development execu-
tive at Bank of America and my first professional boss. We
had previously come to this location to discuss updates on the
JeffVanderLou initiative. Yvonne was both a competent and
compelling leader.

Senator Danforth and I talked for about half an hour,
and he asked about my background, education, and leader-
ship experiences. Despite his stature, there was no air of
intimidation. Instead, I found him to be genuinely kind and
engaging, qualities that would only deepen my respect for
him over the years.

Following the publication of his book *Faith and Politics:
How the "Moral Values" Debate Divides America and How to
Move Forward Together*, Senator Danforth was featured on
Krista Tippett's *On Being*, a program I greatly admired. In this

appearance, he shared insights into his inclusive approach to service and emphasized the importance of serving all individuals, regardless of their faith background. Senator Danforth's commitment to moderate leadership and his ability to bridge differences among people with diverse perspectives have always stood out to me as essential qualities, especially in our current times. This philosophy of empathy, service, and unity resonated deeply with my work at Faith Beyond Walls, where engaging with a wide array of faith communities was central to our mission.

In my role, I had the privilege of connecting with people across the spectrum of belief systems, from Baptists, Disciples of Christ, Methodists, African Methodist Episcopals, Episcopals, Catholics, and non-denominational congregations, among others. I was welcomed into multiple Jewish synagogues—both conservative and reform—to speak during Shabbat services. My engagements also brought me before Muslim, Bahá'í, and Hindu audiences. This diversity of interactions underscored the core of our mission at Faith Beyond Walls: to foster understanding and collaboration among different faith groups and promote a message of service and unity that transcends individual belief systems. This commitment to inclusivity and mutual respect was a reflection of my personal values and a testament to the broader ethos of service that Senator Danforth advocated.

One of my mentors and sponsors was the Reverend Jerry Paul, the founding CEO of the Deaconess Foundation. He challenged me to ease up and not impose artificial limits on my leadership.

"Orvin," he said, "You remind me of me . . . You are too hard-wired. I can see it in your breathing. Slow down. This pace isn't sustainable."

Jerry wasn't just a mentor who shared wisdom; he was a champion who used his influence to support me and many others. As one of my sponsors, he orchestrated opportunities for me, including a board position at the Deaconess Foundation, which primarily focused on children's success at that time. This was one of my initial involvements in a non-profit board. During a breakfast discussion on leadership paths, I mentioned to Jerry that I was content at Faith Beyond Walls and envisioned a long career there. He advised me against speaking in absolute terms at a young age and emphasized that it might hinder potential opportunities. I remember feeling settled, perhaps too settled. Nevertheless, that very day, I received an email about a job opening at United Way.

After joining United Way, Jerry often mentioned that I could succeed him as CEO of the Deaconess Foundation. His confidence in me was a tremendous boost as I navigated the corporate landscape at United Way. Reverend Jerry Paul passed away suddenly on May 20, 2015, following a brief battle with liver cancer, just a year after I became CEO of United Way. I managed to express my gratitude and bid him farewell before he passed, thanks to his wife and longtime friend, Nesa Joseph, who facilitated our final meeting.

Although I was an unconventional choice to lead the major gifts function under the then United Way CEO, Gary Dollar, he took a chance on me. My lack of experience in major gift fundraising didn't deter Gary; he saw potential in my leadership skills. One of Gary's passing remarks that stuck with me was about the need for more than superficial actions to sustain leadership. It's simple for most to show up, mingle, and be amiable, but true leadership demands deeper substance.

I wanted to be a sustainable leader. I modeled my effort after him and worked hard. It was not an easy path, but I became CEO of United Way in Saint Louis with Gary's mentorship and sponsorship. Gary positioned me to be exposed to the right volunteers who, along with him, would determine my future.

After being appointed CEO of United Way, I found myself reflecting on my journey with Gary, sharing thoughts about the pace and ambition that had characterized my career thus far. I contemplated what might have been had I approached my work with just enough effort to get by rather than striving to lead and innovate within our field to establish our United Way as a frontrunner. *What if I had come to work and done only just enough?* I pondered.

Gary, ever a guiding presence, echoed a sentiment that had shaped much of my professional ethos: mediocrity was never an option. He pointed out that settling for average would likely have precluded me from being considered for the CEO role in the first place. My relentless pursuit of excellence, my movement with intentionality and purpose, and my refusal to accept anything less than my best distinguished me. This approach aligned with the vision of the role as described by Jim Buford, the respected former CEO of the Urban League, who regarded the CEO position at United Way as a "lifetime job that was coveted." My commitment to never settling for average, to always push boundaries, and to lead with thoughtfulness and dedication was instrumental in reaching this pivotal moment in my career.

The CEO role at United Way proved to be my most challenging assignment yet. Reflecting on Marylen Stansberry's comment in my early career that "leadership at the top is lonely," I found myself in a solitary period. The organization's business model had long been under threat, and it was difficult for those close to the organization to accept that we were being disrupted by technology and changing donor behaviors.

I believed that my role as leader of the organization was to fully understand the threat and take it seriously. We analyzed the pace of donor erosion, clearly understanding when it would cut into the muscle of the organization and what we needed to do to reposition. This included seeking greater government funding and reimagining the corporate and individual donor value proposition. It was a sobering process. This slow erosion of corporate and individual support was compounded by the rise of social challenges that United Way addressed, exacerbated by income inequality and neighborhood isolation. It became increasingly evident that differences in outcomes related to employment, education, housing, transportation, and the application of justice weren't coincidences or solely the result of behavior; there was a structural component.

In Saint Louis, I embarked on a transformative journey aimed at steering toward a more sustainable business model for our work. This model sought to nurture our existing relationships with numerous corporations while enabling United Way to influence the allocation of funds to projects rather than dictating it. This era ushered in significant innovation through technology integration, program redesign, novel fundraising methods, and increased visibility. One of my mentors, the founder of World Wide Technology, David Steward, encouraged me to push forward.

Concurrently, we faced resistance from individuals and institutions resistant to change, who preferred the predictability of United Way's past operations. This pushback was challenging and prompted deep reflection about whether our focus was attuned to the most pressing issues of our time and whether businesspeople could comprehend that just as they had to evolve in their business, the United Way, too, had to evolve to remain relevant.

This period of introspection coincided with a pivotal moment in our community's history. On August 9, 2014, just a year into my leadership tenure, Michael Brown, an unarmed Black teenager, was shot by police officer Darren Wilson in Ferguson, Missouri. Michael's killing became a catalyst for widespread protests and national discourse. The tragedy and ensuing unrest brought into sharper focus the deep societal fractures around race we were already beginning to discuss as an organization prior to the event. After Michael's death, the Governor asked a group of regional leaders, who became The Ferguson Commission, to study the situation and provide a path toward change.

Against the backdrop of significant criticism, our management and board agreed to serve as the fiscal agent for the effort. By doing this, we received greater visibility and scrutiny for our internal change efforts, which sought to examine our investment decisions through many lenses, including a racial equity lens. Some gestured to publicly show their support but privately struggled with what was required for our region to move forward. Accepting the support role for the Ferguson Commission brought moments of frustration from various quarters. Some donors and stakeholders expressed vehement discontent with our efforts to support the affected communities and misunderstood the reasons behind the protests.

I observed, "Ferguson is the canvas on which people have chosen to paint the picture of their despair," highlighting the broader context of the unrest. I believed that the unrest was ultimately about the lack of freedom resulting from unshared prosperity. I tried to be plainspoken on this issue, often reminding stakeholders and audiences, as I do today, that White and Black people actually want the same things: access to opportunities and shared prosperity.

We were navigating a complex landscape and receiving mixed signals from stakeholders. Some investors pushed to maintain traditional investment strategies and polite conversations, while others urged us to address the contemporary issues unfolding on our streets more directly, both in our investments and the dialogue we facilitated. Amid this, companies that prohibited such conversations at United Way kickoff events stifled my attempts to discuss these urgent social issues.

This was particularly disheartening as Saint Louis faced intense national scrutiny.

I've always believed that the best way to address issues in the national press is through honesty and transparency about where we are as a city and region and by showing a compelling vision for the future. I often said, "How can we turn this crisis into a rallying point for the region?" However, my position as a leader in addressing these challenges seemed undermined by the reluctance to confront uncomfortable truths in private quarters. This collective hesitance to fully engage with the systemic underpinnings of the Ferguson crisis, versus attributing it to isolated behavior, underscored the problem.

Despite the initial surge of goodwill and the flood of promises aimed at rectifying longstanding injustices after Michael Brown's death, there was a noticeable decline in our collective resolve to actively pursue a path toward shared prosperity. While the intentions of many were commendable, the diminishing momentum over time highlighted a challenging truth: the journey toward meaningful change is fraught with complexity and requires sustained, deliberate effort that, unfortunately, seemed to wane as the immediacy of the events faded. What replaces these trajectory-changing efforts is typically a focus on broad based traditional and "safe" charities instead of groups and investment that challenge the economic status quo.

In 2015, I took a significant step in my professional journey by joining the board of Midwest BankCentre, a billion-dollar asset institution. This opportunity came through a key relationship with John Stupp, an understated local business leader whom I met, admired, and worked with through United Way. It marked my first venture into serving on a corporate board. One of my initial experiences in this new role was attending a meeting that included an update on a Department of Justice discrimination claim against the bank. As I sat there, a mix of nervousness and resolve churned within me, culminating in a clear message I felt compelled to deliver: "This can never happen again." The then chairman and CEO responded with assurances, and he labeled the issue as "old news" and promised no recurrence of such events.

Joining Midwest BankCentre's board was both fascinating and challenging. The challenging aspect was primarily due to the maze of regulations banks are required to navigate—a complexity that was new to me. On the other hand, the role was immensely rewarding as I immersed myself in the intricacies of banking. The role was also exceptionally interesting, and it offered me a unique vantage point from which to observe financial deals and consider the community's needs and challenges in a new light. It was eye-opening to see how integral banks are to the functioning of businesses and households. Yet, I recognized that the very communities I was most passionate about often faced the most significant obstacles in accessing banking services. This experience amplified the critical need for financial institutions to serve *all* segments of the community equitably and highlighted the importance of my role in advocating for these changes from within the boardroom.

Today, I serve as the chairman of the board and CEO of this nearly $3 billion bank. I have served on the boards of a university, a global nonprofit, a construction company, private companies, and a public company due to perhaps one of my most meaningful relationships with Jim Berges, the former president of Emerson Electric. When I first engaged with Jim many years ago, it was clear that we were different racially, economically, and in terms of how we think. Through the years, despite all those differences, there grew a profound respect for his journey in life and, I suspect, his respect for mine. Jim has been a tremendous thought partner, mentor, and sponsor. Today, I sit at the intersection of business. That's always the way I've wanted it, but that wasn't always in the cards.

I have lived longer and accomplished more than I ever imagined by seizing every opportunity presented to me. Life is about faith, seizing opportunities, and serendipity. Working at United Way taught me that every breakthrough hinges on the right relationship. We are both shaped by our environment and shapers of it. My journey has never been my plan. I believe that it has always been God's plan. Every step of the way has prepared me for the work I'm doing now, which is focused on giving the most people a shot at winning.

> *I have lived longer and accomplished more than I ever imagined by seizing every opportunity presented to me.*

Throughout the years, I've taken many risks, including leaving a great organization like United Way when I was at the top nationally to take a job in the banking industry where I was unknown and unproven. In banking, experience is valued more than leadership capabilities. If I hadn't relinquished control and followed my plan completely, I would have continued on the path I was already on. However, there was *my* plan, and then there was *God's* plan.

Growing up, greater control to me meant economic security and breaking free from the shackles of poverty that led to the physical, psychological, and sexual abuse I endured as a boy. It was about choosing who I wanted in my universe, my circle, and what I wanted to do with my life rather than being pushed around by those who seemed more powerful. Having greater control was about personal agency—about acting on the world and not simply being a victim of someone else's choices. This sense of control remains the background music to my life, but I have come to rely on my faith in God. I believe He knows best and that most people are inherently good, and I refuse to shape my engagement with the world based on fear.

Today, I have a strong sense of who I am. I'm not as inclined to accept the world's description of who I am or who I'm destined to be. My beliefs form the foundation of my view of myself and others. Those beliefs are not driven externally. What we believe about ourselves is essential to our overall well-being and mental, physical, emotional, and spiritual health. By naming our feelings, we can gain control over them and sustain our attention on our inner focus. I haven't survived; I am surviving.

In the tapestry of human motivation, I've identified five core drivers that resonate throughout our lives. First among these is *money*, which serves as a foundation for economic security and a means to extend sacrificial gifts to others. *Power* emerges as a critical motivator and offers us a sense of control over our lives and the various resources at our disposal, whether human, financial, or otherwise. *Influence* also stands out, crucial for its ability to affirm our significance in the absence of power. It enables us to sway opinions and encourage shifts toward better or new perspectives. *Autonomy* is indispensable because it caters to our deep-seated desires for independence, the pursuit of passions, and the exploration of curiosities. Finally, *connection* fulfills our profound need for intimacy and meaningful relationships, both with others and the divine, and lays the groundwork for lasting memories that imbue our lives with meaning.

Our self-perception is intrinsically linked to our sense of worth and shapes our understanding of overachievement versus high achievement. High achievement, I've learned, is not about racing through life's checkpoints but embracing the quality of the journey over its speed. This understanding has enriched my roles as a husband, father, and leader and allows me to prioritize the essence of living over mere efficiency.

The truest form of love extends beyond what others feel for us—it's reflected in the divine love that embraces us and the love we harbor for ourselves. Early in life, resentment and anger toward those who should have protected me led me to construct emotional defenses that shielded me from vulnerability. Yet, despite the absence of regret, I've sought reconciliation, particularly with my siblings, and hope that my children and wife—my steadfast support—recognize the depth of my love and appreciation.

My current material circumstances stand in stark contrast to the impoverished environment of my childhood. I now have the privilege of choice and a platform to advance ideas that are important to ensuring shared prosperity, including the neighborhoods I grew up in. Despite transcending the physical confines of my childhood communities, the energy I derive from them and the connection I have to them remain strong. My commitment to uplifting those communities will never wane.

My journey has also led me to appreciate the essence of living life to the fullest. No longer do thoughts of ending my life cloud my horizon as they did when I was a child. Instead, I focus on living abundantly, cherishing each moment, and seizing the opportunity to make a meaningful impact. This shift toward a life rich in purpose and connection underscores a journey not just of survival but of profound transformation and growth. I have also come to value functional relationships, having learned their importance in college and in life.

I've transitioned from a background marked by adversity to becoming one of the few successful Black CEOs in the banking sector, not only in my home state of Missouri but across the nation. I believe that my success means that more doors can and should open for others.

When I stepped into my banking role, the questions came in torrents. People were skeptical about why the bank would choose me, a Black man and, perhaps more crucially, someone without banking experience, to lead it.

"Was it affirmative action?"

This question was familiar to me from my college days. People were curious—or concerned—about my motives and questioned how this new path aligned with my extensive background in social services and whether I was selling out. My response has always been clear: my career in social services, culminating in my role as CEO of United Way of Greater Saint Louis—the largest and most innovative United Way affiliate in the nation when I left—was driven by a commitment to stabilize lives and foster social mobility. The move to Midwest BankCentre was a strategic decision to magnify my impact by facilitating broader access to financial capital for communities traditionally sidelined by the banking system.

Having been in this top position for over five years, I have demonstrated that my appointment was not about affirmative action or selling out. I understood, as I did in college, that I needed to perform, and I understand who I am and what I represent, no matter what level of success I achieve. This was about affirming that effective leadership can mirror the broad diversity of America—and that's exactly what we've achieved, delivering both shareholder and community results.

Today, as the Chairman and CEO of Saint Louis's second-largest privately held bank, I find myself in a unique position, navigating diverse spheres and embodying what many thought was impossible given my background. This role has shown me that we can tackle many societal challenges by democratizing access to opportunities and capital. I am both inspired by the potential for progress and aware of the persistent systemic barriers. It is clear that a collaborative effort between government, nonprofits, and businesses is essential to close the opportunity gap and drive meaningful change.

In an era of significant wealth disparities, while the inclination might be to rely more on charity, I view this as a critical moment to shift from historical wounds to shared prosperity through equity, justice, and economic empowerment. This is the same type of empowerment that Annie Turnbo Malone experienced when local and national communities rallied around her, helping her achieve what was once deemed unthinkable and unimaginable. Her legacy continues to impact lives today, with seeds planted long ago still bearing fruit. Wealth creation, in its essence, is about ensuring that everyone has a fair start—not predetermined by racial or socio-economic factors but by their individual capabilities and efforts. Our collective future hinges on our ability to influence systems, policies, and practices toward more inclusive growth.

Entering the banking industry highlighted the challenges of breaking traditional molds. A year before my transition, a survey conducted by *Bank Director* talked about the homogeneity of the banking sector with few, if any, Black CEOs at the helm of mainstream financial institutions. That is why I see my journey not as a personal triumph but as a step toward broader systemic change as I advocate for diversity and inclusion at the highest levels of financial, civic, and corporate board leadership.

I want people to see their potential in my story, to understand that it's possible to navigate and master the systems that surround us, and to use their unique experiences as a steppingstone toward achieving greatness.

However, that's just one facet of my journey. Beyond breaking barriers in the banking world, my life encompasses experiences that resonate on a deeply personal level. My time in the foster care system, childhood dreams of being like Superman, and overcoming numerous challenges along the way are what I hope will inspire the younger generation. I want people to see *their* potential in *my* story, to understand that it's possible to navigate and master the systems that surround us, and to use their unique experiences as a steppingstone toward achieving greatness.

What truly enriches my life is the opportunity to mentor others and show them that every story, no matter how fraught with adversity, holds the power to propel us forward. It's about turning our trials into triumphs and using our narratives not as anchors but as engines of change and platforms for achievement. My ambition is to be a living testament to the idea that our backgrounds do not define us; rather, they equip us with the resilience and determination to forge paths that others might follow. This legacy of empowerment and possibility is what I want to leave behind. I want to encourage others to see beyond their immediate circumstances and envision a future where they, too, can achieve remarkable feats.

My life has been a blend of relentless hard work and the fortunate serendipity when I crossed paths with those who saw potential in me and chose to believe in me. The concept of serendipity often sparks a debate about the balance between divine orchestration and the autonomy of free will. While some grapple with the notion and think that a higher power predestines our every encounter (rather than an exercise of free will), I hold a nuanced view. I believe that divine providence and free will can coexist harmoniously. God grants us the freedom to make our own choices, but that doesn't negate the role of serendipitous encounters in our lives. Instead, while we navigate our paths through free will, the opportunities that arise—seemingly by chance—may well be divinely inspired. However, it's up to us to seize them.

This doesn't dilute the essence of hard work or relegate the concept of serendipity to either mere luck or favorable breaks by a fortunate few. Rather, it acknowledges the intricate dance between our efforts, our choices, and the unexpected opportunities that life presents. This blend of our actions and serendipitous connections propels us forward. While we steer our ship, perhaps the winds that fill our sails have a divine touch.

When I looked inside, I realized that God was indeed present in me. I needed to do my part and let God guide my steps, all while practicing patience as His unconventional plan unfolded. This journey led me to become known as the "Accidental Banker." Yet, I could not have reached this milestone without overcoming numerous obstacles: surviving beyond the age of twenty-eight, navigating life's myriad challenges, receiving unwavering support from dedicated champions, mentors, and sponsors, and carrying on the generational faith passed down to me like a precious family heirloom. As I approach the age of fifty, I do so with increased peace, wisdom, and confidence. Filled with immense joy and emotion, I continue to lean on His word. From the protective shadow of His wings in Psalm 91 to the promise of His unwavering presence in Joshua 1:9, the Bible's assurances of God's constant companionship have always brought me comfort. Reflecting on these promises during my darkest times, I have experienced an indescribable peace, even when faced with seemingly insurmountable circumstances. Now, as I stand here as *Twice Over a Man*, I am vividly reminded that we are never alone, no matter the battles we face.

TWICE OVER A MAN

Here I stand, at last, more than twice over a man,
Fear is no longer the dominant cast, though still prominent in
the plan
The plan has been survive, forgive, to reach twenty-eight was
ideal
Each year that takes me past that point, can be best professed
as surreal

It's surreal that I forgave,
After all but hope had been taken away my development was
surely delayed,

I coped without notice of the Spirit dwelling within,
Fortifying my position and belief, subduing grief, making
faith my friend

The plan was significance not just to outlive,
But to reshape a spirit of timidness, and remake our families
shield

Shield from the land that sought to snatch potential from the
womb,
Shield from the molesting hand seeking to permanently entomb
Shield from the man who tells you who you are, and
Instead of lifting your sights on all to behold, keeps you
focused on the scar

Shield from impoverished thinking, abundance is the goal,
Shield from the brokenness, a stronghold that exacts its toll
Shield from a mindset, already set to fail,
because you've not yet seen success from among the place
you hail

Becoming anything means always overcoming
I wake often still wondering, when life's clock will stop
A preoccupation of sorts with life and death, another
    optional plot
Though focused on the here and now,
Memories are constant and tears fall down
My past is still very much afloat
Despite my effort to submerge it will not drown

It's not sorrow I borrow just for company sake
It's a permanence of sadness that comes with trauma that
    makes it an irreplaceable trait
But sadness isn't the end, there is joy to be had
And I have had plenty of joy being husband, provider, and
    dad

I have had plenty of joy finding purpose to this life, I'm
    climbing, clinging to the things that matter most, supplant-
    ing defeatism with a different host

I often think about you mother and wonder if you're proud
    of the man that I become to date as You watch me
    through the cloud
As I navigate my way through life I wonder if it was you
Who instilled in me a faith so strong and the will to see life
    through

Here I stand at last, more than twice over a man,
With a shield of protection from God above so
The next generation can . . .

ACKNOWLEDGMENTS

I extend my appreciation to all the people who came in and out of my life to mentor, sponsor, and give me a hand up. They believed in me when I didn't believe in myself. I am grateful to the business leaders, authors, and civic leaders whose lives and works inspired me and to the countless individuals who have contributed to the rich tapestry of my life. To the professors who inspired me, the staff of Emergency Children's Home and the Disciples of Christ, the staff at Annie Malone Children's and Family Services Center, the Missouri Division of Family Services workers, and those who pray for me daily, like my godmother Carmen Charleston. To my childhood friends, especially Lamar and Ronell—you were like brothers to me, and no amount of time will change that. To my sister Carmen and brothers Antwon and Cornelius, love can be misunderstood, even when it still stands. All counselors and those who are affectionately known to me as my "day ones" were ground zero in helping me become the human I have become.

I would like to express my deepest gratitude to my wife, Latriece, who sat through my brainstorming sessions over the years and listened to every chapter, whether she wanted to or not. She provided feedback that guided the stories I told. I want to thank my friends the MOCHAs, and I'm also extremely grateful for Nancy Erickson, editor, whose insightful feedback and guidance shaped this manuscript into its final form. I am also indebted to Tim Fox, whose early research, writing, and recordings helped capture many of the stories and the historical narrative that is in the manuscript. I am grateful to the board of United Way of Greater Saint Louis including leaders like Rich M, Mike D, Michael M, Kimmy B, Anne B, Donald S, Larry T, Jan H, Hugh G, and others who were consistent in their support during my service. I am grateful to the board of Midwest BankCentre for their commitment to a more inspiring bank mission that includes value creation for shareholder and the community and to my colleagues at the bank who provided feedback on the memoir and who I get to do this powerful work with. A heartfelt thanks to Michele Holton for her thorough analysis and heartfelt feedback.

Special thanks to my city, Saint Louis, for giving me so much love. I believe we can and will be better for all people. Let us never forget that efforts to promote shared prosperity is our race to the top. To my family for their unwavering support and encouragement throughout this journey. I am grateful to my friends for their understanding during my periods of absence and obsession with writing. I am grateful to the Stupp family, particularly John Stupp, for choosing his words wisely when asked what he thought about me leading the bank. He replied, "It might be interesting." All the people in my life have made this an interesting journey.

ABOUT THE AUTHOR

Orvin Kimbrough, a husband, father, and man of faith, has navigated a remarkable journey from a challenging childhood in East Saint Louis to a prominent role in Saint Louis's financial sector. His early years were marked by adversity; he was raised by a single mother in a community gripped by poverty and drug issues. At just eight years old, a pivotal moment occurred when he discovered his mother had passed away from a drug overdose, which propelled him and his siblings into the foster care system. This initiated a tumultuous two-decade journey through institutions like the Annie Malone Children's and Family Services Center.

Despite formidable obstacles, Orv viewed education as his ticket out of poverty. Against the odds, he not only completed his education in Saint Louis Public Schools but also obtained undergraduate and graduate degrees in Social Work from the University of Missouri-Columbia, a Master of Business Administration from the University of Missouri-Saint Louis, and a Master of Arts in Theology from the Aquinas Institute of Theology. His career stands as a testament to his commitment to unleashing human potential.

As the chairman of the board and CEO of Midwest BankCentre, Saint Louis's second-largest locally owned bank, he has significantly broadened access to capital for local families and businesses. Under his leadership, the team has set records in profitability and efficiency and have grown the bank's assets to nearly $3 billion, with operations spanning seventeen locations and in all fifty states through its digital channel.

Before his banking career, Orv dedicated twenty years to the nonprofit sector. As president and CEO of United Way of Greater Saint Louis, he steered the organization to become the nation's largest affiliate, raising nearly $80 million annually. Since joining Midwest BankCentre in January 2019, he has been a driving force behind Impact Banking, an initiative encouraging institutions, foundations and high net worth individuals to leverage a portion of their balance sheet for the benefit of the underserved in their local community. He also committed the bank to lend an incremental $200 million over five years to support historically underserved communities.

Orv's insights and leadership have been featured in major publications like CNBC, *Fortune,* and *CEO Magazine.* He is also an active community leader, serving on the boards of numerous significant organizations. He has served on the board of United Way Worldwide, was the board chair of Missouri State University, and is currently a member of its College of Business Executive Advisory Council. Additionally, he serves on the Federal Reserve Community Depository Institutions Advisory Council (CDIAC) and is one of nineteen commissioners on the National Academy of Medicine's Commission on Investment Imperatives for a Healthy Nation. Beyond these civic roles, he has also served on the boards of a construction company, a private financial services company, and a Fortune 1000 public company.

Orv is a member of the Young Presidents Organization, Alpha Phi Alpha, and Sigma Pi Phi (The Boulé)—both holding the distinction as the Nation's Oldest Black Greek college letter and post-college Greek organizations, respectively.

Celebrating more than five years with the bank, Orv's guidance has propelled Midwest BankCentre to record growth and differentiation. His life and career inspire hope and perseverance, underscoring the profound impact of unity and community support in achieving collective well-being.

For more information, go to https://orvinkimbrough.com.

Printed in the USA
CPSIA information can be obtained
at www.ICGtesting.com
JSHW072231021024
70987JS00001B/1